From Survival to Thrival™

How to catch the boat to your
successful, thriving life
(even if you thought you'd missed it)

© 2009

by

Kathrin Lake

Library and Archives Canada Cataloguing in Publication

ISBN: 978-1-926626-79-6

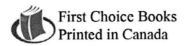 First Choice Books
Printed in Canada

Front cover design by Rivera Design Group, Vancouver, B.C., Canada

Table of Contents

For Jim,

My dance partner and life partner

who teaches me about love every day

I would like to thank Gail Buente and Jim De Haas for helping me edit. I would also like to acknowledge friends, family and associates who have lent me their stories and experiences. Mike Schell, Darren Wride and John Hawkins for their advice, and Elena Rivera McGregor and her talented team for the cover design.

Chapter One - Are you ready to thrive?

If you are reading this book, no doubt it means that you want to change your life. You want more money, a terrific mate, a better job, you want a home, a vacation, you want to overcome fears, be decisive, have joy in your life, and you want to do things that make you feel great. You want to stop just getting by and start feeling that you have life by the horns. Alright! Good for you. You want to move from just surviving to thriving!

So, how do you do it? How do you make things change in your life? How do you make things better? No matter how much debt you are in, no matter how many times your heart has been broken, no matter how many jobs you've lost, how long you've been out of work, or how much you've procrastinated on big decisions, no matter how many dreams have fallen by the wayside, or how many times you've wanted to check into the psyche ward… you want to turn a corner. And, if you've gotten through all that and are opening up this book, the good news is there is still great hope for future success. You <u>can</u> turn things around. You can bring happiness, joy, success and even prosperity into your life.

But when I say you can bring all those things into your life, keep in mind that life does not change – people do. Life will do what it has always done. Other people will do what they have always done. The government will do what it has always done; the economy will still have ups and downs; your family will respond the way they always have; and your co-workers will respond the way they always have. Nothing about the way life works will change. People change their lives by making changes to their attitude and their habits. So, this begs the question: are you ready to thrive?

Don't worry; you don't have to answer that yet. This book is going to take you on a journey, and on this journey you will want to confront the only person who makes a difference: yourself. And that's not easy. What this book will do is give you some valuable perspectives that most people have either never been taught, or don't fully understand. Because they don't get it, they find they are not where they had hoped to be, even when things "should have" worked out.

Perhaps you are feeling bitter, beating yourself up for making "stupid choices" or for not being able to see what was coming, or being weak or scared, or for "pissing it all away", for being in the wrong place at the wrong time, or for "not being where you thought you should be by now." And here you are stuck in an uninspiring job, or broken-hearted again, or unemployed, living paycheck to paycheck, or on the dole, or living back at home, or waiting for the check to come in. Or, you are saddled with responsibilities that you resent, or you're not doing what you love, or are just unhappy and not knowing why, or a combination of any of these things plus a few other obstacles, challenges, addictions, or problems. No joke. Life can be tough.

Often I hear people misquote Darwin and say that "life is survival of the strongest," or "only the strong survive." In fact, what underpins Darwin's theory of evolution is the observation that those best able to adapt are those best able to survive... and thrive. Therefore, an important key to thrival, as I call it, is the ability to adapt or change. When looking at accomplished people's lives, biographers will often note that the individual was able to remake themselves or overcome great disappointments or obstacles by adjusting. These individuals will often diligently experiment, trying to find the right fit or the right thing that works until others notice. This takes a kind of strength, but not aggressive strength. It takes persistent strength. But, for persistence to work, it has to be coupled with adaptability. People who are able to make adjustments while staying true to themselves are the ones who survive and seem to enjoy the journey. These people have used their obstacles to better discover who they are. One could say that they were not only adapting to the world, but were stripping away old trappings to become more of who they are. As Shakespeare said, "To thine own self be true."

Being a human resources consultant and working with managers and entrepreneurs for many years, I have been in numerous situations where the manager or owner wanted an employee to change. One day, we had an issue with an employee whose attitude and behavior were out of line. The employee was put on probation for thirty days. I said to the wise manager, "Do you think he can change in thirty days?" The manager replied, "I'm giving him only one day to change; the other twenty-nine days are to prove it."   This reminded me of when I was teaching writing and I used to ask my writing students if they thought Scrooge, in Dickens' *A Christmas Carol*, was realistic. Could people change their behavior overnight? This always spawned an interesting debate, but I am inclined to agree with the wise manager, change can happen quickly, but maintaining it is the hard part.

At the beginning of Dickens' classic tale, we see that Scrooge is rich, but miserly with his money. He is not well thought of, has severed his relationships and he is suspicious of others. He has lost his capacity for compassion. He does not indulge in any comforts, though he can well afford them. Scrooge is a wealthy man but he is surviving and not thriving. By today's standards, this description of Scrooge may even indicate the first signs of mental illness. It is only later, after his magic night, that he begins to truly thrive and enjoy a meal, a joke, other people, and children. He can even enjoy a sneeze.

The story I told about putting an employee on probation is a realistic occurrence in everyday life. In fact, all human resources professionals, me included, have frequently had to document employees being put on probation and facilitate the meetings. The message in these meetings is we expect change or there will be consequences up to and including termination. Sometimes it works, although rarely to mutual satisfaction. Sometimes this results in the employee's difficult decision to quit, or in the employer's difficult decision to terminate. Often the employee will pull themselves up by their boot straps for awhile, but will slide back into old habits after a few weeks. Almost always, somebody feels someone else is to blame. The manager feels it is the employee, the employee feels it is the manager, and the people in HR graciously conclude "it wasn't a good fit."

Rarely has anyone come into my office out of their own free will to say to me that they want to make themselves a better team player and to ask if I can help them do that. People will take many things to a crisis point before they admit that they may have to change, and even then, they often can't or won't be able to maintain it.   People in 12-step recovery groups frequently talk about hitting rock bottom. That's when things are so bad that a person is in such a crisis they either have to change or risk losing their family and friends, their health, their career, their possessions, and sometimes the breath of their own life. Some people literally risk it all, before forcing themselves to change. If you are in a 12-step spiritual recovery program, stay in it – nothing I will say will be incompatible. It is my sincere wish that most people will not have to reach rock bottom in order to make positive changes in their lives.

So how do you make changes that really count, and continue to count? The fact is, strength, confidence and luck are temporary for everybody. Yes, confidence too. It is only people who can be mutable and remake themselves who continue to do well no matter what happens. The tragedy is, people want things to change, but they do not want to change their actions, attitudes and perspectives. They are set in their ways. They are unwilling to change. They think *that's too much work!*

Telling people that "change is work" scares people away and yet it may surprise you to learn that many of the changes that will move you toward thriving will seem infinitesimally small. They will not seem like things that could possibly change your life. And yet, they are not at all small. In fact, small is the best place to start and some personalities have a hard time accepting that. The smaller a change is, the easier it is for people to believe they can maintain it, and so they tend to be more successful. For example, what would I say was one of the small things that changed my own life? Was it changing careers? Starting a business? Losing weight? No. Those were all the big, visible changes that everyone saw me make. It was actually only the small things that I alone knew about, which had an impact on me daily and made a difference to the person I had chosen to be. One such small but enormous change was noticing and adapting what words came out of my mouth. I will relate some stories about how much difference that makes, but there were also changes that seemed even less significant that were very important.

I was thirty-eight years of age before I made my bed daily. You may chuckle because, for a great many people, making ones bed isn't seen as a significant change in their daily lives, let alone in becoming a success. Some people may wonder what kind of slob I was anyway, but others may respond to what I revealed, guiltily admitting to themselves that they also frequently forgo making their beds before starting their day. Frankly, I had a problem with procrastination that I still keep on top of to this day, except it is no longer a problem, and it no longer keeps me from living a rich life.

I remember going into a counselor's office for a first appointment and the counselor asked me what brought me to her. I told her that I was afraid. She asked what I was afraid of, and I said everything. I said, "I'm afraid of washing my dishes, I'm afraid of making the bed, I'm afraid of paying bills, I'm afraid of doing my taxes..." What I was trying to say was that I was anxious, and procrastinated because of it. My first step was to admit that what I was feeling was fear, and this fear surrounded everything I did. Other significant portions of this book will have to do with fear, procrastination, and creating healthy habits in a healthy way. Managing your fears, however, is not about finding someone to tell you what you should do. The changes that a person chooses to make (and maintain), be they small or large, are personal and significant to them, but they will also expand outward like the concentric ripples of a pebble tossed in a pond, having a far-reaching effect.

Some people seem to be addicted to big changes in a way that keeps their lives chaotic. Perhaps they frequently change addresses, friends, vocations or partners. If you think you fall into this category, in any part of your life, my question is: do you feel that you are truly thriving this way? Perhaps you do. Perhaps your definition of success is never to be bored and to keep moving. You may feel the inevitable sacrifices are worth it, or you may simply not be able to see any other way.

Some people believe change is not within their control. Things just happen to them. This is the same thing as asking life to change. Things may happen, but if the same type of things consistently happen to you with similar results (either negative or positive), trust me, it is not life that is doing it to you. Life has the same kind of fabric for everyone. Mark Twain once said "Don't go around saying the world owes you a living. The world owes you nothing. It was here first." In effect, he was saying life doesn't work for you, it doesn't gang up on you, and it doesn't decide to shine on you. Life just is. What you choose to do with life is how you reap rewards. The only important question to ask yourself is why did you pick up this book? Are your reasons important enough to make you look at how you are doing things now, and to make some adjustments? Most people have already decided that their reasons are important, but even with the knowledge of how they might adjust, people often struggle with maintaining their new ways. We need to do a deeper assessment of two things: how changes are made and how we think of success.

For all of us, success may mean describing similar feelings of satisfaction or happiness, but success ends up looking as diversely different as the individuals we are. Before I focus on how people change, how they become successful and remain successful, or how they move from surviving to thriving, I want to define what success is. And what does it mean to thrive? For that matter, what does it mean to survive? Examining these ideas in the following chapter is the first step on the road to understanding success and thriving. By the way, I prefer that you read the first four chapters together and after that, feel free to peruse the table of contents and skip ahead to chapters or exercises of interest. But for now, I welcome you to the yellow brick road towards thrival.

Chapter Two - Defining Success

I had an epiphany one day after I had broken up with the man I had convinced myself was the love of my life (we can all be quite convincing despite the facts). I remember I was in my bathtub, sobbing and feeling miserable. I had no job, I was in debt, and a few weeks earlier my apartment had been broken into and I had no insurance. I was sobbing mostly because I was coming to terms with the fact that after four years of trying to make it work, my relationship wasn't happening. In this depressed and traumatized state, a thought occurred to me: would I be this miserable about breaking up with my beloved boyfriend if I had my finances together? If I was out of debt and I had a good income, would I be quite this depressed? I was surprised to realize the answer was no. I would not be as upset if I was financially thriving. I realized that I couldn't change my ex-boyfriend – lord knows I had tried – but I could change my financial situation, if I chose to focus on it. What I knew then was that I never wanted to be financially shaky again. It was my Scarlett O'Hara moment.

My apartment being broken into also seemed to hold a message for me. The universe was trying to tell me something about my own security, or lack of it. I had not made myself secure either physically, financially or emotionally. And slowly, steadily, that is exactly what I achieved. It took time and was successive process, but once I knew how to do it, it progressed steady and easily, and put me on what I call the upward spiral.

What is Success?

If I ask the question, *What is success?*, right away one could start writing lists of how to define it and that's great, but whenever I want to define something I look at the words I have chosen and investigate their original definitions. So let's start there, with the word success. The origin of the word success/succeed from Old French means to "go next to them" or "getting near to something." It was only later that it evolved into the Latin form that meant "doing well" or "prospering." We still use the word succeeds and succession to refer to the next in a line of monarchs, holders of office, or holders of roles in a corporation. To say we do things successively means we move toward it in steps, gradually, replacing the old with the new. When you reflect on the fact that the old word form of success is a process, as opposed to a product, your perspective can change quite a bit. That is one very important notion to keep in mind when moving from survival to thrival. Don't Confuse Process With Product.

Process over Product

One catchy saying that was in vogue for awhile was "Life is what happens while you are making other plans." This statement is another way of saying that life is a process but we try to make it a product. We want it to be about the things we want to have happen: goals. Don't get me wrong, goals, plans and dreams are terrific and I recommend making them, but if you are not going to enjoy the journey to get to them, you will not enjoy life and you will not be thriving.

When I ask people how to define success, they will often say having money, having time, having freedom, or having something else, like a home or a good job. Does "having money" sound like a process or a product? When the verb "having" is attached, it is not a process. It is an end product. A process sounds like: training every day, in all kinds of weather so that I can compete in half marathons and marathons for as long as I can. A process sounds like: I will maintain my health by eating healthy foods daily, exercising weekly, and keeping informed about good health. A process sounds like: starting and maintaining a business that I feel passionate about, and want to continuously learn more about.   A process sounds like: learning how to manage and maintain my finances and make ongoing, calculated, smart financial decisions.

The mistake most of us make is to define an end product or goal without defining the process to accomplishing it. To move toward thriving, not only do we want to define that process, we also want to see ourselves as doing that process happily, or at least with moments of satisfaction.   That means building in milestones or finding the satisfaction tasks or moments. I have heard that people sometimes build in rewards for themselves as in, if I write five pages today I will allow myself a treat. That may work for some, but it is better and healthier to find moments of satisfaction within your process of doing what you are trying to accomplish. And if you can't, if your goal or task is merely a means to an end, then perhaps a check mark on your to-do list may suffice. Or, if it means you get bragging rights, that's great. But for longer, ongoing processes, you will want moments that are satisfying within the process itself.

I never thought I was a very organized person, but I discovered that the organizing parts of projects are the relaxing and de-stressing parts for me. Now, I look forward to those parts. In my process of writing, it often means I have to produce text before I can organize it, so I have a built-in reward and motivation. Another reward for my writing is my enjoyment of the feverish pace of writing down words when I am hot on a trail. Since I know that typically happens anywhere from ten minutes to half an hour in, I remind myself of that before I begin. Otherwise, I can easily lose my incentive for getting down to it.

When I used to be a runner, I would look forward to the part in the run where my pace felt like I was floating, and my thoughts got very clear. It is all these satisfaction moments within a process that we should remember when setting goals, and perpetually remind ourselves that it is these moments, and not the grander end goal, that brings us satisfaction.

If you have a process that on the surface seems like deprivation, as in controlling your diet, then you'll want to create and find positives in that. Some people enjoy the rituals of cooking and eating. They slow down, savor their food, and sometimes create a candlelight ambience. I enjoy shopping for fresh foods, and I give myself permission to spend more on healthy foods and spices that I haven't tried before. When eating out, I also enjoy the challenge of picking the healthiest things I can find on the menu and still have a tasty, lavish meal. I also had a very important tip from my Weight Watchers' team leader which was to enjoy the feeling of hunger pangs that you choose not to give in to. She suggested that it is healthy to keep in touch with our feeling of hunger and be able to distinguish between the feeling of hunger and going hungry. Likewise, people can take pleasure in recognizing that they have had enough to eat before they feel uncomfortably full, and being aware that they are dehydrated and thirsty for water instead of craving a sugary drink. By reconnecting with your own body, you can turn the negative thoughts of hunger and deprivation into a positive aspect of your process. Awareness of these positive aspects to your process will help you to move successively toward your goals without being too attached to an outcome. Outcomes are things such as your weight on the scale, or how thin you look. Some of these goals we know can be both unhealthy and harmful, but if you remember process over product, you will move toward thrival.

Right now, think of a goal you want to accomplish and try writing it as a process. Find the positive satisfaction moments you know you will enjoy within the process that are not attached to the outcome. Read over the example below and then write one of your own in the blank spaces provided.

Process Goal: To enjoy the process of slimming my body – which I have verified by an expert is overweight for my height and age – by eating healthier foods and controlling my portions.

Positive Satisfaction Moments:

- ☐ Allow myself to buy new products that are high fiber and try more foods I know are healthy
- ☐ Allow myself to stock my crisper and fruit bowl with my favorite fruits and vegetables
- ☐ Rise to the challenge of healthy choices on restaurant menus
- ☐ Know that the feeling of hunger that may be there before I go to bed, or during the day, is a way of reconnecting with my body
- ☐ Recognize the difference between hunger and thirst – know when I may be dehydrated for water
- ☐ Enjoy recognizing when I am satisfied and when I should stop eating before becoming full or uncomfortable

- ☐ Buy a rice cooker (used or new) and buy different kinds of high fiber rice
- ☐ Allow myself to buy a filtered water system, carry a water bottle with me, or have a beautiful glass pitcher of water, and drinking glasses in my office
- ☐ Notice and write down positive changes to my body and my health as I go through this process

Exercise

Process Goal:

_____

_____

_____

_____

Positive Satisfaction Moments:

☐ _____

☐ _____

☐ _____

☐ _____

☐ _____

☐ _____

Got Happiness?

I've talked about how an awareness of process is important in successively changing and ultimately in thriving. I've talked about how you can define the processes of goals to make a difference, but let's go back to what it means to thrive and succeed in your whole life. For the general purposes of this book, I want to define your purpose in life in two ways. Let's say your purpose in this life is to be happy and healthy. That means as happy as possible and as healthy as possible most of the time. To that end, you can create many goals, but in order to remain happy it is advisable never to get confused that achieving your goals will, by themselves, make you happy. They might, or they might not. What I know for sure is that if you believe that achieving goals alone will make you happy, and you don't achieve your goals, you are going to be unhappy. Not because you didn't reach your goals, but because you chose to link happiness with achieving those goals. This may seem like a subtle twist but it is very important to understand how it operates in people's actual lives.

Who is Thriving and Who is Not

I went to university with a young, intelligent, creative man who said that he must write a best-selling novel. He told me that he would not be truly happy until he achieved this. Toward this goal, he isolated himself, wrote and wrote and wrote, and finally finished a first draft of a novel. I had to admire his discipline, but when he networked with other writers and editors, which was not frequently, he didn't always choose wisely who to go to for support. I noticed two things. He became suspicious of those who did truly care, and he was very critical of others' work (an example of victim mentality, which I will cover later). He may have written a novel but he really didn't have a clue how to sell one, or how to adapt to a marketplace. This is not uncommon for writers, but most realize that if they need new knowledge, they have to seek it from those who do know. As he struggled, mostly alone, it did not take long before I could see clearly that the goal he had set for himself was also making him miserable. As it turned out, the young man became very depressed and fell victim to mental illness. It is a chicken-or-egg question to me whether his choices brought on his mental illness or vice versa, but in any case, I have seen many others take a similar route with their lives.

The ironic thing about this story is that I think he really did enjoy the process of writing, but he certainly did not enjoy the process of sharing it, which was in contradiction to his dream. He was fixated on a product – having a best selling novel. But worse, he had directly linked this to his happiness, and also dangerously linked it to his self-worth. And when it was not happening, there was nothing left for him but to despair, complain, criticize and blame others and detach even further.

Writing is one process, getting a book published is another, and marketing a book as a bestseller is another entirely. But, even if he had all the skills, or had taken his novel to the right people, and had been a bestselling author, would that make him happy? If so, would he have to produce another bestseller every time he wanted happiness? That would mean long stretches of time without happiness. He may have been like Scrooge, before his transformation, with "success" behind him but no idea of how to truly thrive. In order to thrive, he could have started to focus on how to be happy along with his achievements. Not only would he have to love the process of writing, he would have to learn to enjoy the process of sharing, and even aspects of selling. And even if he couldn't do that, he could have started to focus on personal happiness independent of his goal. The underlying lesson is that achieving goals may be satisfying, but they do not give you ongoing happiness. If the purpose of your life is to be healthy and happy, you might achieve your goals, but still feel you are not thriving.

Another well known ironic success story is Howard Hughes. Hughes was an innovator and a risk-taker extraordinaire and always had new projects and goals to move toward. In the end, however, he was alone, dealing with mental health issues, imprisoned by his own successful trappings, and alienated from people. Notice how his story and my university friend's story have common themes about physical and mental health and their importance beyond ambition. The process of maintaining a healthy mind, body and soul is one of the greatest keys to thriving. That said, to me health also includes financial health (as my epiphany in the bathtub taught me), but financial health does not have to mean the riches that our society likes to flaunt in front of us. Not to sound too much like a TV commercial for a financial institution, but financial planning for stability, security and peace of mind is simply a sensible program to include in your life. It does contribute to maintaining your health, which, as the old cliché says, has to be number one.

The stories of Howard Hughes and my university friend may have had tragic ends, but I want to stress that reaching for goals can be a great thing, if you keep it in perspective. Don't make yourself miserable expecting to get something that you may or may not be able to attain. En route to your goals and dreams, surround yourself with attainable joys. Why? Because the routes to goals and dreams will always go sideways. Or, as a wise woman I know likes to say, "If you want to make God laugh, tell him your plans." This isn't an admonishment against planning; it simply means you are wise to learn to enjoy the processes life offers you, without being attached to outcomes. All this amounts to is: dream, enjoy the process of moving toward your dreams, but expect those plans to go off track, and be persistent anyway. If life did not go off track there would never be serendipities or fortunate accidents. Going off track can put people on track. People who are too tied to their plans often miss opportunities that are calling them. I will speak more about this when we look at the myth of focus.

Got Attitude?

I heard a very successful writer say that if she gets to write and can make a modest living, then anything else is cream. That writer is Elizabeth George, a writer who has received more than a little bit of cream with a large number of published mysteries to her name that have achieved acclaim and a wide audience. Yet her attitude has always remained the same. I once saw her argue with a prominent New York literary agent about this. He suggested that at the heart of every author was the desire to make the bestseller list (a product not a process), but she insisted that she doesn't give a fig for bestseller lists, and that writing is a more important process to her than that. George started as a teacher and successively became one of the highest regarded teachers in her State, being awarded for her work inside and outside the classroom. She exemplifies someone who loves the processes of life, but has also gained further success. She had taken the risk of changing and adapting and had "moved to the next thing" (Old French for success) by taking on a very different life from that of a teacher. She enjoys her cream, but that is not the foundation of what makes her life rich. What makes her life rich is her attitude.

Another example of a different successful attitude comes from the great Canadian sprinter, Bruny Surin. During the 2000 Summer Olympic Games in Sydney, Bruny Surin, a gold medal contender, had injured himself in the earlier qualifying heats. Despite days of rest, Surin declined to race rather than risk further injury. When asked during an interview about the difficulty of that choice, Surin was surprisingly calm and said it was an easy choice. While most sprinters live for the one chance in four years - that one goal of proving themselves at the Olympics – Surin felt he had already achieved a greater gift. He was a beloved father, husband, and family man; a successful business man and a pillar of his community and his church. He had chances to coach and had other hobbies and ventures on the go. The choice was easy because, for Surin, maintaining his health, happiness and life were far more important than the dream of Olympic gold. This is someone who does not confuse thriving (a process) with a goal like an Olympic medal (a product). This story reminds me of John Candy's character of the bobsled coach in the movie, *Cool Runnings*, based on the true story of the first Jamaican Olympic bobsled team. In the movie, he tells his young protégé how he nearly ruined his career by cheating. "I had to win." he says, "I'd made winning my whole life. And if you make winning your whole life you have to keep on winning." He sums up this hard-learned lesson by saying, "A gold medal is a wonderful thing, but if you're not enough without it, you'll never be enough with it." Bruny Surin already knew this.

Other success stories remind us of the Old French meaning of success which suggests "moving toward the next thing." What drives many great creators are the challenges and obstacles that stand in the way of their vision. While they can be let down or devastated if a project doesn't reach fruition, or even feel let down when it succeeds, most truly successful people move on to the next challenge, passion or interest. Failures or successes, don't stop them. They show a keenness to be connected to the processes of life.

Pop star, Madonna, has had cross-generational success by changing, growing, maturing and by letting others influence her. She seems to work with each new world she finds herself in. I have often thought of Madonna as she first portrayed herself, a Marilyn Monroe sex symbol for a new generation. But Madonna, unlike Marilyn, had a strong sense of self and faced the realities of being a sex symbol with confidence and control. She seemed to be Marilyn Monroe getting revenge. No treadmill for her. Madonna is, and always was, fully in charge of her own image. Unlike Marilyn, Madonna took her image of beauty and youth into middle age and motherhood without losing her sense of self. If you had to say which of the two women were more successful, you would again spark that debate on how to define success. Is it dollar values? Lasting infamy? Greater happiness? Longevity? That is why the question of what success is has to precede any question of how to get there. People often make assumptions which lead them somewhere that they thought they wanted to go, but which turn out not to be what they imagined. While the journey toward achieving success can be very valuable, without introducing a balanced attitude it can have results as tragic as Marilyn Monroe's death. This is why I argue for thinking of success as a process that always leads you to happiness and health, or as I like to call it, thriving.

It was another famous tragic death, that of Princess Diana, that made me think again, how easy it is to get muddled about what success is. In fact, that is part of the process: Get It Wrong Before You Get It Right. The day after Princess Diana died, my local newspaper published on the front cover, along with her well-known, glamorous visage, the year of her birth and death. I remember this part distinctly because the year of her birth shocked me. It was the year of my own birth; we were the same age. One day before, she had wealth, fame, children, beauty, a magnificent wardrobe, a new-found lover, and at the time, I had not one of these things. But suddenly it seemed to me that I was lucky, I was the one who had everything, because I had the one thing Diana did not have: my life.

Although Diana had a classic woman's fairytale of having it all, the nightmare had been revealed. Simply marrying a prince was not all it was cracked up to be. Bulimia and depression revealed a lack of self-esteem that is essential to the health and happiness of any human being. Tackling these issues, changing her own self-image, and stepping down from being a princess was what made her start to thrive. Though we will get it wrong before we get it right, unfortunately we only have a limited amount of time to start straightening it out.

Ordinary People

I don't want you to get the idea that I think only famous people are successful. Many of us can think of people around us who we consider to be thriving. Take a moment to think of some. Ask yourself why you believe that. What are the reasons you feel they are thriving? Are the reasons valid? Or did they simply make different choices than you have made? In my definition of success, many people I know, and you know, are successful. When I meet a person or a couple who have a thriving mentality, I notice a number of things. First, they are happy and generous. They tend to be people who read, and have educated themselves formally or informally. They tend to be people who connect well with other people and have a loyal and diverse group of friends. They tend to be healthy for their age in mind, body and soul. They tend to have a well organized home and they have made it beautiful. They have interests and activities, and they love what they do for a living. They tend to be people who would describe themselves as part of a community, and they give back to their communities. They are wise, with a strong sense of values and ethics, yet they are not quick to judge others. They are people who are aware of themselves and their faults. They are positive people who see their life journey as filled with ups and downs, but can still enjoy that journey. They tend to be people who enjoy counterpoint and dialogue about issues. They tend to be effortlessly proactive. Frequently they are humble people. Others are drawn to them and feel tenderness toward them. Notice that I did not mention material wealth, business success, fame, or status. Though they may very well have those things, it is not essential that they do.

Do Your Thing, Do It Well and Share It

Mahatma Gandhi, Mother Teresa, Dian Fossey, Martin Luther King and many others were martyrs who lived and died for causes. You may not identify with any of those individuals but if you look around, there are always local heroes who are not trying for fame or fortune. In my home city of Vancouver, I was always impressed with a local hero, Joe Fortes, a humble man who lived near English Bay beach in the early days of Vancouver and became it's the city's first self-appointed life guard, rescuing over 100 people from drowning and teaching hundreds of kids how to swim. In recognition of his service, the Parks Board gave him his own bungalow by the beach where he remained until late in life, continuing to be a friend and teacher to the children. What may be more remarkable, he was one of the few black men who lived on the West Coast above the 49th parallel at the turn of the century and overcame the common place fear and prejudice of all the people he chose to befriend. The fact that the community embraced him, and that today numerous monuments exist in his honor shows there are many ways an individual can succeed and thrive. Joe Fortes simply did what he loved and did it well. He shared of himself and he was persistent. That's all. Persistence is a key. Sooner or later, actions and attitude are rewarded, because it makes a difference.

What makes you happy?

As I suggested before, the only reliable definition I have for success is health and happiness, therefore, I have had to figure out what makes me happy and healthy, and then make sure I included it in my life frequently. It also means recognizing that one's attitude can create or destroy one's happiness.

One idea for an attitude shift is to think smaller amongst your larger dreams. In other words: Always Set Yourself Up For Success. Make sure you fill your life with slam-dunk happiness that feeds the sacred trinity of your mind, body and soul. Personally, I have at times felt so desperate and bad about myself and my life that I have stared at other people, assessing them from their outward appearance, and thinking to myself, "I'd rather have that person's life." I used to torment myself by obsessing over get-rich-quick schemes. Occasionally, that way of thinking pops back into my mind, and I realize quickly that I am making myself miserable. I have to go back to doing what makes me happy. What do you do now that makes you happy? Are you doing it enough? How can you be consistently happy?

There is both an art and a science to happiness. First, the science. Serotonin is a natural hormone in your body. It is a neurotransmitter involved in the transmission of nerve impulses. Your body manufactures the amino acid tryptophan, which increases the amount of serotonin in the brain. Serotonin, among other chemicals, helps maintain a "happy feeling," and seems to help keep our moods under control by enabling sleep, calming anxiety, and relieving depression. We know that food, drink, sleep and physical activities all affect serotonin levels. We also know that if we make a habit of being happy – a natural happy – the easier it is for our brains to produce and maintain serotonin. Studies about laughter and health have shown that the release of laughter can produce serotonin, regenerate the body, and reduce hypertension and stress levels.

Look at the following list of natural happiness boosters, check off those you do and add some of your own Make a note of the ones you would like to do more often.

Exercise

✓ What Do You Do?　　　　✓ Do You Do It Enough Or Not Enough

- ☐ Reading
- ☐ Hugging
- ☐ Laughing
- ☐ Dancing
- ☐ Singing, alone or with others
- ☐ Playing an instrument
- ☐ Gardening
- ☐ Running or other active exercise
- ☐ Team sports
- ☐ Yoga or other restorative exercise
- ☐ Participating in events or performances
- ☐ Cooking healthy food

- [ ] Storytelling
- [ ] Feeding others
- [ ] Walking in nature
- [ ] Being with good friends
- [ ] Playing with children
- [ ] Hanging out with others who share a passion, hobby, art form or career
- [ ] Following a career, passion, hobby, or art form for the enjoyment it brings me
- [ ] Going to the library
- [ ] Teaching, coaching or mentoring
- [ ] Playing or working with a pet or animal
- [ ] Making love, caressing, sex (alone or with another)
- [ ] Recreation of any kind
- [ ] Being out of doors in nature
- [ ] Resting, reflecting, or meditating
- [ ] Doing hobbies
- [ ] Playing games
- [ ] Writing (in a journal or for others)
- [ ] Talking to interesting people
- [ ] Listening and asking questions
- [ ] Telling jokes
- [ ] Volunteering
- [ ] Joining groups

- ☐ Soaking in a bath or hot tub
- ☐ Being in the presence of great art: music, movies, visual art, performance, etc.
- ☐ Spiritual practices
- ☐ Other:
- ☐ Other:
- ☐ Other:
- ☐ Other:

I'll say it again, goals are great and it is important to have dreams, but it is also important to fill your life with that which makes you happy and healthy on a consistent basis. Life is what happens while you are waiting for something else to happen. Whether or not you try to do it all, you do want to enjoy yourself. Your life is a process and you have control over it, in both small and large ways. And the small ways are the most plentiful, so start there.

Non-Nurturing Quick Fixes

Below is a list of things that are immediate gratifiers but are non-nurturing in the long run. You should try to keep them to a minimum. Quick fixes, as I will call them, do affect your body chemistry and can affect your ability to produce serotonin, and give you a happy feeling. While drugs that are depressants (alcohol), anti-depressants (Paxil) or stimulants (coffee) can give you a high feeling of happiness for awhile, they can also deplete your serotonin levels and can reduce your body's own ability to produce serotonin and other hormones that help you balance your moods. Studies about anti-depressants published in Psychology Today[i], have found that a high percentage of placebos given to patients who thought they were taking anti-depressants, reduced or eliminated their depression as well as did the actual anti-depressants. This was particularly true in young people and was attributed to two factors. The first was that the longer you have depression the harder the road back, or put another way, the longer you have negative mental habits, the greater chance you are worn into the rut of depression. So, the young have a greater chance than older people to help themselves; and even with placebos had the same success rate as with anti-depressants. But, the second factor was that during the clinical trials the young people received one-on-one attention from adults that had been missing from their lives. And, in another more recent study[ii], they found through control groups that mothers who were at high-risk for postnatal depression, reduced the chances of developing depression by 50% if they had heart-to-heart talks with peers on a regular basis. Later on, under health, we will talk again about the importance of positive interaction with others as a part of good mental health. When you are older it is harder to change well-worn ways, and therefore more support from others to make new habits is recommended.

Regardless, the case for natural highs being able to help people better perpetuate happiness is a strong one[iii]. So it is important to be aware of your quick fixes and not substitute them for the things that make you truly happy. From the list below, check off some of your quick fixes. Do you consider any of them self-destructive?

Exercise

✓ What Do You Do?   ✓ Do You Do It Excessively?

- ☐ Comparing yourself to others frequently
- ☐ Watching TV, Video, or DVD
- ☐ Time on the computer, especially computer games
- ☐ Smoking
- ☐ Drinking alcohol
- ☐ Drinking coffee
- ☐ Using experimental, prescription, or illicit drugs for highs
- ☐ Hurtful or unsafe sex, sex that is void of emotion
- ☐ Depriving yourself sexually
- ☐ Over-eating consistently
- ☐ Under-eating consistently, anorexic and bulimic tendencies
- ☐ Over-exercising consistently
- ☐ Under-exercising consistently
- ☐ Shopping to excess, whether buying many small cheap things, or spending beyond your means and going into debt
- ☐ Overeating Chocolate
- ☐ Overeating Sugar and Saturated Fats
- ☐ Self-abuse or staying in abusive situations
- ☐ Abusing others, verbally (by being critical), or dominating and manipulating others, or being physically abusive

- ☐ Falling in unrequited love, or in a relationship where one person is much more in love than the other person, or being obsessed with one person
- ☐ Worrying excessively
- ☐ Being reclusive
- ☐ Being a workaholic
- ☐ Not being able to make commitments to work, friends, lovers, etc.
- ☐ Spreading yourself thin with too many activities, or flitting from one thing to another without commitment or focus
- ☐ Any emotion i.e. anger, love, hate, fear, anxiety, sadness that one can indulge in excessively. (Yes these are quick fixes, although not always pleasant. For some they are a habit which distract them from enjoying life and working on true health and happiness)
- ☐ Time in bad company: when lonely, you consistently choose to be with others who are depressed, self-absorbed or non-nurturing, often trying to help them instead of looking after yourself
- ☐ Time spent blaming others and complaining
- ☐ Other:
- ☐ Other:
- ☐ Other:
- ☐ Other:

These quick fixes are not evil, and if you do indulge in them, as everyone does from time to time, it does not make you a bad person, or a person destined for depression or addiction. I am not interested in judging you. No shame, no blame. In fact, I don't believe you can live a truly full life if you don't have some improper fun and debauchery. In fact, if we did not have those bad habits, writers would have nothing to write about and there would be no great art. It is the human condition. It is life. In this stage of your life however, you may want to consider trying to put everything in proper measure. You are reading this book for a reason and we've already established that you're here to thrive, which means less pain and a lot more consistent happiness. To that end, it's probably more fruitful for you to focus on doing more of the things that make you happy (the first list), than to immediately try to forgo all of your quick fixes. That said, it is important to start to be aware and understand the mechanics of quick fixes even if you aren't going to stop them tomorrow. Some of them may be biggies that you will want to look at and that we will get to shortly under Elephants. For now, you are going to want to start working on your mental shifts. How do you think of success? How do you think of yourself? And how do you start giving yourself things that are good for you?

Although you can try to use quick fixes as a substitute for true happiness, if any one of these things, or a combination of them, forms a major portion of your life, this could spell trouble for you. As we now know, many of these things can either indicate or lead to chemical or emotional imbalances, and even mental illness. They certainly won't lead to fulfilling happiness when they are the backbone of a life. When you indulge in these things to excess, which is a tricky thing to gauge at times, it does not matter how much money or traditional success you have (think of Princess Diana), you are surviving, not thriving.

The Upward Spiral

These non-nurturing practices, if unchecked, can put people on a downward spiral. What keeps people on that downward spiral, or in survival, isn't news. Using the adage "attitude is everything" one can always identify the people who are perpetually on the upward spiral, and those on the downward spiral. Even if you think you have a great attitude, I am going to challenge you to look deeper at your expectations of life and yourself. For right now, it is enough that you start to view the idea of success differently and begin to learn the art of happiness, the art of thriving. This is the beginning of the upward spiral. People experiencing the upward spiral are not demigods or blessed, they are people who have the ups and down we all experience, but these individuals, will again and again:

▸ Have a consistently positive attitude

▸ Have consistently healthy habits

▸ Be able to look at the reality of their situation – no denial allowed

▸ Be able to adapt plans, goals and habits

▸ Be able to admit when they are wrong or unsure

▸ Look at failed attempts or mistakes as learning opportunities

▸ Genuinely like or love themselves

▸ Look at the positive in others and try to nurture it

▸ Be able to risk actions to reach goals, change habits, or gain knowledge

Hopefully this chapter has helped you to rethink success, or reminded you of its truer meanings. In the following chapters we can further break things down to help you get to the success I call thriving.

To recap this chapter:

☐ Success is successive, an on-going process of making changes.

- For the purposes of this book, we are going to define success as thrival as optimal happiness and health (incl. financial health)
- Process over product. Define all your goals as the processes by which you accomplish them, and note what the in-process satisfaction moments are.
- Don't stop having goals and dreams (products), but don't tie goals to happiness (process).
- Give yourself slam-dunk happiness without over-indulging in quick fixes.
- Be conscious of whether you are practicing the attitudes and practices of the upward spiral – see previous page.

Chapter Three – Your Attitude, Your Everything

Do You Control Your Attitude, Or Does Your Attitude Control You?

In theory, we all have the ability to change our attitudes, or reframe past failures so that we can see opportunities and learn from them. However, theory is only theory and most people have a profound difficulty changing their dearly held beliefs and attitudes. Change of this kind does not happen overnight as Scrooge's did, but it is forged with a strong commitment. This happens on the heels of an event that is either wonderful or traumatic or both.

When something bad or good happens, it creates an opportunity to make a mental change, say yes to something new, make a better choice or put behind us the things we are hanging on to unnecessarily. Until a mental shift is made, opportunities often don't manifest themselves. For example, until I believed that losing weight was not about dieting, looking good, being skinny, starving myself, fitting into smaller sizes, or even being in shape, I could not keep my excess weight off. My weight ping-ponged for over twenty years but most of the time I was at least 40 pounds overweight. The attitude that worked for me was that losing weight meant maintaining my health. It is all about health. I maintain a healthy weight by weekly moderate exercise, eating better foods, and keeping my intake proportional to my exercise - note that this is a process. My attitude shift also led to getting rid of that which I no longer needed to carry around. In addition to my fat reserves, I realized that I no longer needed to carry around my hurt feelings for a past relationship, which, like the overweight body, threatened my mental, emotional and soulful health. It was important that I made a conscious choice that I had had enough pain and wanted to change my attitude about health, love and relationships.

But for all human beings it often takes pain and trauma to motivate that shift. However, it is important that it be the right pain and trauma. In regards to body image, for example, you don't want the pain that motivates you to change to come from other's disapproval of you. You may think you don't do this, but it is so ingrained in our society that it is very difficult to avoid. Like many women, and men, I would try to diet, exercise and lose weight every time I had a bad relationship experience, or wanted to look like the people in magazines. That was the wrong pain to use for motivation. It was when I started to recognize that I was having chronic, recurring, painful health issues that I found the right motivation. I started to investigate my health with more seriousness and the issue of diet became more apparent. At the same time, two traumatic events involving loved ones gave me learning opportunities. My father had a heart attack and a close friend had cancer. Before I go further, I will say that both survived, recovered and are doing well. However, at the time I was naturally worried about them. Near-death experiences of yourself or of loved ones will naturally start you considering your own health and mortality.

I was a lot like my Dad, especially in my eating habits. We both had eyes bigger than our stomachs - which were not small - and cleaned every crumb off our plates, unable to say no even when we were full. We also loved fatty and high-carbohydrate foods. I could also see these habits in my friend who had cancer. I decided to do research to see what foods a cancer patient should be eating in recovery. By accident, I found out something that surprised me.

Although I associated unhealthy eating habits with heart disease, I had not associated it with cancer. What I found out was that the likelihood of getting almost any cancer was more strongly linked to being overweight than either genetics or environmental factors. Needless to say, the research I did on diet started to change my attitude about weight loss and maintaining my health. More importantly, it made me conscious that I would need to become proactive if I wanted to turn my survival life into a thrival life.

Near-Death Experiences

As I said, the near-death experiences of those close to me moved me to change my attitude, and I am certainly not alone in that way. Some time ago, I participated in an intense storytelling course. Our leader asked us each to tell a story about a turning point in our lives. It took a few days to tell all the stories and the experience was quite amazing. We noticed that about three-quarters of the stories involved near-death experiences, including my own. In these near-death experiences, each person made a commitment to change that marked a turning point in their lives. Like Scrooge, they did literally change overnight. In fact, it is the visit from Scrooge's final Spirit, the Spirit of Christmas Yet To Come, which shows Scrooge both Tiny Tim's death and his own death. Prior to that moment Scrooge had been saying to each spirit that he was too old to change, but only when he is left weeping on his own grave stone does he fully repent and say "I am not the man I was," and promises that he will change.

The problem, of course, is that, like the rock-bottom experience of 12-step group members, a near-death experience is a harsh way to learn how to change your attitude. You cannot manufacture these experiences. Or can you? As the heading of the previous section asks, Do You Control Your Attitude or Does Your Attitude Control You? The answer is: both. The whole intent of Dickens' story is to teach people to take full accountability for their actions in life, because after death it is too late. Unfortunately, people aren't interested in what they can control until they can feel the pain in their own lives. Part of changing your attitude is being aware that there may be pain in your life and you may be living a life of survival. You will also want to help heal the pain in others' lives but you may want to do something about your pain first, so that you can effectively reach out and lead others.

Are You Living with Some Kind of Pain?

Telling someone that they need to change rarely works. We are not built that way. One of my favorite quotes used in my course on procrastination comes from an expert on the phenomenon of task-avoidance, Dr. Joseph Ferrari, who says, "Telling a chronic procrastinator to 'just do it' is like telling a clinically depressed person to 'just cheer up'."[iv] It is important that people come to their own awareness, as Scrooge was forced to with the help of the Spirits of Christmas. Awareness is often accompanied by pain but awareness is the first step toward Success and Thrival. The first things a person needs to be aware of are that they are, in fact, living with pain and that they don't want to. Pain in a life -- physical, emotional or otherwise -- is intermittent. Because of this, as strange as it might sound, most people choose either to apply temporary solutions or prefer not to see their intermittent pain as warning signals that they need to make changes. In other words, if you ask people on a bad day if they are living in pain they will say yes, but catch them on a good day, sometimes less than 24 hours later, and they will tell you they are just fine, thank you very much. Often the rock-bottom syndrome is the only true wake-up pill, but many people will never get there because they stay on a perpetual roller coaster, without acknowledging the real problems, and therefore they do not take action. To beat the roller coaster you have to start nurturing in yourself an attitude of *self-awareness* combined with *accountability*.

The Elephant in the Livingroom

Some people acknowledge that they are in need of some kind of help or healing without acknowledging the obvious. They look in vain for a rescuer, focusing on their past lives, or using psychic charlatans or other distractions from the real issues. This is denial. This is the elephant in the livingroom that is difficult to look at. Just as thriving requires maintenance, any kind of pain, lack of health, feelings of failure or of being stuck –any survival or victim mentality - requires you to keep choosing attitudes that keep you stuck in that place. If you have been using Tarot cards and Psychics for years, for example, and you still feel you are not thriving, it may be time to set them aside. You can go back to them later if you want to, but it may be time to try being practical and grounded. If this scares you, offends you, or makes you angry, consider that it may be your hot button. If it is your hot button then it is also your elephant. Elephants are big. They are not small, like the changes I was talking about earlier. Elephants are often obvious to everyone else but you. Elephants are: You are in debt and ignoring your financial situation. Your weight is contributing to your health problems. You have a terrible job you hate which doesn't pay you enough. You are addicted to substances. You are underweight, anorexic or bulimic. You are experiencing mental health issues. You have low self-esteem. You are obsessive about a beloved who does not return your affection. You refuse to make important decisions about your career. You never finish the things that you start. You are obsessed with past experiences. You are lonely but refuse to make friends for fear of rejection or because you don't know how. And on and on. These are not near-death rock-bottom experiences. These are life experiences. But they are still big.

I once knew an AA member who had had the near-death rock-bottom experience. He said to me that it is easy to choose death, you can choose it at any time, but it is much harder to keep choosing life. The attitude is not only to choose life, but to choose to thrive with joy and happiness. Choose a rich life. Part of that is to recognize what *causes* you genuine pain and rid it from your life. This is as important as finding what causes you joy and including it in your life. In order to do that, you have to name that elephant. Naming a problem correctly can give you the great power of knowledge and understanding. For example, I have known people who did not understand what was happening to them. They couldn't face certain things in life. As a result, they just felt bad about themselves. Eventually, they understood that they were experiencing depression, and in some cases they found out it was something that ran in the family. Other times it was anxiety. One woman finally figured out she was experiencing PMS symptoms that included mild paranoia. With that knowledge, by giving it a name, she was able to recognize that it was manageable. She could control it by diet, exercise and awareness. It was influenced by certain thought patterns. With research, focused exercises, new habits, and support, you are able to counteract many of these things. For other less physical problems like debt control, or being a shopaholic, you have to be able to name that problem and stop hiding from it.

Once you have named your elephant, you are going to want to look at your elephant with quick glances to begin with until you can stare at it directly and be comfortable calling it by name. You have to stop identifying with it and realize that while it is a part of your habits, it is not part of you. Just a choice. There is no shame, no blame and you do not need to feel bad about the elephant. If you have more than one elephant – and we frequently do – try to look at only one at a time, or they may overwhelm you. You are not going to do anything, for now, you are just going to look. Looking at your elephant can start with a trip to the library or the book store.

I used to read lots of books on relationships. Even when I wasn't in a relationship, I would read books on relationships. I thought that relationship problems were my elephants. Wrong-o. Remember, an elephant is what you don't want to look at. Your elephant is 100% yours. With relationships, I could always rationalize that it was someone else's fault, not just mine. To thrive you need to take an attitude of hardnosed self-awareness and accountability. What were my true elephants? I did not want to look at my health. I did not want to look at my finances. But when I started getting down to it, I started looking at my weight first, but I failed because, as I've stated before, I wasn't fully connecting it to health. Instead, I was connecting my weight to my relationships via my self-image and my self-worth. In other words, out of low self-esteem, I believed I was unlovable because I was overweight. Low self-esteem would turn out to be a bigger elephant for me.

Fortunately, I did start looking at my finances. Thanks to a friend who nagged me to read a popular book on finances, I bought the first book I had ever read on the subject. I still thank my friend heartily. I did need, however, to have my crisis in the bathtub before I could really succumb to my friend's suggestion. People around you sometimes do know what's good for you. They see your elephants. And, the ones who love you see your elephants without judging you. They just want you to be out of pain. And I do too.

The self-awareness of those first steps and taking the recommended advice made it possible for me to get my finances back on track and create a plan for the future. But I had a few more elephants to look at. Fortunately, now that I was aware and had decided to look these things square in the eye, I discovered that there were many resources to help me. I will mention these resources as I move through this book and also in the section called *Firing On All Cylinders*. To begin with, however, books were my most valued resource.

If you feel you've already tried using books, but you still are not getting anywhere, it is crucial to find out why you are falling down. It could be that you haven't yet found the right information for you. Keep looking. It could be that you are afraid to implement the things the experts suggest. Are you procrastinating? If so, maybe you should research procrastination or fears, some of which I have already talked about, and will explore in the chapter on *Fears and Habits*. Do you still refuse to change your ways, but expect life to be different? Sorry for the bitter pill, but life is still

going to have its ups and downs. Maybe you need extra help.
Some of you will thrive best with those one-to-one lessons that
only experts, professionals, teachers or coaches can give you
before you can feel you are the skipper of your life. This is covered
in *Your Health Plan* chapter under *Health for Your Mind*. There is
help, but you are going to have to face the fact that only one person
is going to rescue you: you. That is why this is under the chapter
on your attitude.   The attitude that we are talking about is
accountability, but accountability can be tricky in one critical
respect: the blame game.

To have a thriving attitude, to be accountable, you must face your
elephants <u>without beating yourself up</u> or feeling that there is
something wrong with you.   There isn't. Being told there was
something wrong or bad about you may have resulted in your
challenges now, including physical challenges.   You may have
absorbed false messages from society about where you should be
and as a result feel a profound sense of failure. Even if you were
not told directly there was something bad or flawed about you, you
may have drawn the conclusion that there must be. If there wasn't,
surely you would be happier and better rewarded by now. That is
the rationalization. But, there isn't anything wrong with you. And
you do have what it takes to be out of pain and live a much
happier, healthier, stress-free life, no matter what has happened in

the past. You do have everything it takes to thrive. A major part of that is to keep choosing the thriving attitudes and lose the just surviving ones.

Victim Mentality – The True Evil?

One thing I can say with certainty is that if you have a victim or blame/shame mentality – and I mean people who blame and shame themselves - you will stay stuck in survival. You will continue to battle unhappiness and dissatisfaction, or even continue further down the downward spiral. In other words, if you decide that you have no control or little control, you won't. Being a victim means blaming others for your woes, wanting it your way, blaming yourself, and telling yourself you have no or little control. It is the most damaging attitude of all.

"Victimhood" is where thriving is not possible and even surviving can be difficult. If you want to know about such conditions, I recommend reading about the concentration camps in World War II. More than one concentration camp survivor, most notably psychologists Viktor Frankl and Bruno Bettelheim, witnessed that even in situations where people seemingly had no control and did not have any of the opportunities we have to thrive, they were able to choose an attitude that helped them to survive. If they chose the attitude of victimization and hopelessness they would, with certainty, receive that fate. Those who survived often chose to continually reconnect with the view that they would survive and that they had things worth living for. Survivors would recognize moments of beauty, power, or triumph, however small, and give them merit amidst all the brutal, sickening and disheartening torments they had to endure. Those who survived resisted in small ways the victim mentality. Even though they clearly were victims, they chose a different view. They did not beg for mercy, but they did ask for help. The difference was, they didn't count on getting the help they asked for. When they were chided or abused for asking, they were not surprised. They took it, and they still asked without begging. Because they asked without complaining, pleading or needing it, Bettelheim found they were more likely to get the help. These were the ones who survived. If people can have that attitude in those unspeakable conditions, then what can we do with all the freedoms we have in our lives?

In contemporary life, how does a victim attitude affect us daily? We are not living in the despair of a concentration camp, but many of us have created our own self-limiting prisons. Let's go back to Scrooge for a moment for some clues. In an excerpt from *A*

Christmas Carol, the Spirit of Christmas Present shows Scrooge the two children under his robe, clinging to him.

"Look here." *From the folds of his robe he brought two children; wretched, abject, frightful, hideous and miserable.*
Scrooge said: *"Spirit, are they yours?"*
"They are mankind's... This boy is Ignorance and this girl is Want. Beware them both, and all of their degree, but most of all beware this boy, for on his brow, I see written Doom, unless the writing be erased..."
"Have they no refuge nor resources?" *cried Scrooge*
"Are there no prisons?" *said the Spirit, turning on him for the last time with his own words, "Are there no workhouses?"*

I have already discussed how Want, or pursuing goals and only goals while ignoring the things that make us thrive, can make us miserable. Ignorance is choosing to ignore or be unaware of ourselves. Two more children, similar to what Dickens revealed, cling to most, if not all, humankind. They are called "Denial" and "Blame."

If Dickens were here today, I think he might well be happy, perplexed and appalled. He would be happy that there are no workhouses in first world countries, but perplexed that our prisons are still filled with the poor. He would applaud our compassionate social programs, but would be perplexed that people still live in poverty on the street.

Part of Dickens' confusion comes from a misunderstanding of the complexities, but also a misunderstanding of victim mentality. When speaking with social workers of all kinds (and working with a street child myself) I began to realize that while we can provide shelter, programs for growth, role models, caring and love, we cannot ultimately help those who continue to have an attitude that they cannot help themselves, despite receiving this aid and support. When people cannot acknowledge that they can help themselves, but instead remain passive, victimized and childish, any progress can feel like one step forward and three steps back. For people on the street it clearly has cruel origins beyond poverty alone. It often stems from childhood abuse, mental illness, Fetal Alcohol Syndrome or other difficulties. Many individuals have literally missed whole chunks of what we would consider normal childhood development. On the streets, in order to withdraw from pain, they begin drug habits; addictions that further stunt their growth.

The strange thing is, there are many of us who are not living on the streets, who are not addicts, who are not suffering from any of these afflictions of the homeless, but who nevertheless exhibit the same kind of behaviors and symptoms. Many of us have to face that we may still have that deadly attitude, or victim mentality which harbors ignorance, want, blame and denial.

While victim mentality can mean blaming either yourself or others, victim mentality is also the ability to sabotage yourself, by creating conditions and excuses instead of going forward on a commitment. I remember the story of an employment counselor who had been working with a client to help get him back to work, but the client always had an excuse for why her suggestions were not going to work for him. After exhausting many resources and trying for weeks, fed up, she finally said to him, "Just give me a simple yes or no answer. Do you want to work?" The client was silent for a second or two and then answered, "Yes...but..." The "but" was his demise. More conditions and excuses followed, but she refused to let him rail on about them. This was his victimhood hiding in the little word "but." Denial is to hope for a perfection that does not exist. Mark Twain's idea that the world owed him nothing was foreign to this client. It is important to seek help and ask for help, but if you have not cast off your own chains like Jacob Marley's ghost, you will continue to carry a heavy weight of powerlessness and no amount of support will propel you forward. Yes, sometimes you should hold out for better things and know your worth; that is high-self-esteem thinking. But there must be a balance. If you are not even taking effective action toward moving forward when the situation clearly calls for it, then it is likely that you are in some sort of denial. You are in victim attitude.

It is also important to know the difference between genuine blocks and manufactured ones. People can come up with an excuse for everything. We can rationalize. We blame. We say why it won't work. If someone has tried something before, then they might be able to say why that method genuinely will not work for them. They know the down side of that method. But often people will say no before they say yes, without having given the proposed method a shot. Because it usually involves effort, discomfort and sacrifice, we tend to reject it right away.

All important choices, even small ones, are going to involve some sort of sacrifice, but many of us often stay like street people in a cocoon of childhood where we want some other larger adult-like body to intervene and make it easier: the government, your boyfriend, your company, God, your parents, your wife, anybody but yourself. Why? For two reasons. One is that people are frightened of the unknown. They have chosen to stay children, unable to face adult life alone. We will talk more about fears later. The other reason people cling to powerlessness is that somewhere inside they have decided that it is their right to be taken care of. The truth is they don't want to grow up and take care of themselves. Even though we may not have wound up on the street, many of us have missed a part of development, which led us to have misplaced expectations about life.

Victim mentality will come out in all of us as soon as we develop what is known in Human Resources as "entitlement." While some employers can be accused of exploitation, some employees can be accused of having a sense of entitlement far and above what is healthy for them. In other words, it is very easy to expect the company to take care of you, or to blame management for all sorts of things rather than believe you have some control over your own issues with your work. And if the work conditions are so unacceptable, despite ways you have tried to be proactive and provide solutions, ask yourself why you are staying. If you are waiting for management to change, or other people to change, you could wait forever. You are not ever going to thrive in your workplace if you do not take some responsibility. You could take some positive actions that involve your making changes too, even if the action you must take is to leave.

While a victim attitude may affect big things in your life, like your job, I want to look at the small things you deal with daily to

understand how this mentality holds you back. It is nearly
impossible not to assign blame to things outside ourselves.
However, we often blame only after setting up an expectation of
entitlement in our minds well in advance of anything going off the
tracks. In other words, we pave the way for our disappointment
and our disempowerment.

I myself feel I have a sense of entitlement about a great many
things and I attach myself to them rapidly. I have a sense of
entitlement about parking spaces and often say, "that's my spot."
Then, just as I make a turn to get it, someone else swoops in, and I
find myself very pissed off. I had developed a sense of entitlement
that quickly. If you have children, you will inevitably notice this
in their sharing, or lack of sharing. Children quickly develop a
sense of entitlement and can get pretty touchy when they discover
they don't have entitlement. They also learn that sometimes they
can get what they feel entitled to if they keep whining.
Unfortunately, like street people and children, there are always
parts of ourselves that develop an unhealthy sense of entitlement,
and we do like to whine. One of the laments I hear from unhappy
adults is their disappointment as to where they are in life versus
where they thought they should be by now. This is one of their
personal mythologies. I will talk about personal mythologies later,
but they often involve entitlement, and this comparison to where

you thought you'd be is a common one. Sometimes they blame themselves, the economy, the government, or simply life itself. But essentially, they have developed a sense of entitlement for a future that did not pan out the way they thought it should. However, if you ask them questions about their lives, often you find that they have accomplished some pretty interesting things. They have traveled, met interesting people, earned degrees, or have knowledge of subjects that few others have. Yet, despite their choice to explore their sense of self rather than be career-minded, or to have education rather than buy real estate, or to be a traveler rather than settle down, they somehow think they should still end up with a life they chose not to lead. At the same time, lots of adults on the other side have the car and the house, the relationship and the kids, yet lament that they have never traveled, were never educated, or have never done anything exciting. Someone else's grass always seems greener than our own. When you probe further you know that these individuals had opportunities to choose other things, but they chose not to lead. They either refused the other path outright when it was possible, chose not to make a sacrifice, or simply didn't bother to pursue what they now lament they don't have. It often seems that people just want to be disappointed with life or themselves. They want to stay in victim mode. That's where Zen teacher Cheri Huber says, "Rather than having what you want, it is better to want what you have." Notice that wanting what you have, means you have no need to feel that you are entitled to something you don't have. You are not bitter.

Sometimes people did risk getting into an investment or a particular field or career at an unfortunate time – I know I have – and we did not see any fruits because of reasons beyond our control, like economic forces. Frequently these adults show regret. They talk about their lives as if the game is over and there is no possibility of making changes that may fulfill whatever they feel is missing. They feel they are behind the eight ball and they will never catch up. They felt entitled to something that didn't happen. Rarely do people have a back-up plan. Only the thrivers choose an attitude that keeps them open to all future possibilities.

Have you ever caught yourself thinking or saying things like, "If he doesn't come through on this, I am never going to give him a heads up ever again," or "If I don't get this promotion I'm just not going to care any more," or "that bad decision ruined me for life." Try monitoring what you both say and think. See if you have a built-in victim-maker attitude inside you. The more you recognize it in yourself and understand that this attitude is keeping you stuck, the better off you are.

"If I don't get the promotion, I am going to ask why and listen to what they have to say, because it may be valuable to me as I build my career. I may want to make some changes."

I do occasionally hear this forward-looking, courageous mentality, but not often enough. I remember once being very candid with an internal job candidate that one reason that she did not get the job was that the other candidates were very clear in their career direction. I told her that they knew why they wanted to go in that direction, they had talked to others in the field, and they knew what skills they wanted to bring to it. Instead of taking this knowledge as an indication that she may need to ponder what she really wanted out of her career and what her strengths were, her first reaction was to focus on the fact that we had hired an external candidate instead of an internal candidate. She accused management of not being sincere in their policy to give opportunities to people within the company. Well, the opportunity was there, but it is what you do with it that determines the end results. I was trying to help her grow and get clear in her career direction. In retrospect, I wonder if it would have helped to try harder to give her a clearer message, but at the time, her attitude was to blame and perhaps nothing could have got through to her. I only hope that with further reflection she did develop her career direction. But I know that she did share a lot of bitterness talking to others. That did not help herself or the company; it was a lose-lose situation. For the record, I can also give many examples where a manager also had a victim attitude by making an individual, or individuals, scapegoats for their own poor management practices. In either instance, people cling to those two attitudes of humankind's desperate children of "blame" and "denial" and rarely nurture "accountability without blame" and "awareness."

How can a person nurture accountability without blame when it seems natural to blame? When something goes wrong, most of us give ourselves two options: blame myself, or blame someone or something else. In psychology, they call this locus of control. Some people have a tendency to blame things inside their control (i.e. themselves) and others have a tendency to blame things outside their control (e.g. the economy, the bus was early, no one told me). The folks who blame things outside their control are usually the ones who are more deeply entrenched in a mentality of powerlessness because they have chosen to believe that nearly everything is outside their control. But those in the first group, who blame themselves, can walk a thin line of victim mentality too. They may realize they have some control but what they choose to do with their control will determine the extent of their victimhood, or their freedom. If they choose to beat themselves up with self-blame without taking account of the outcome of their actions, then they too will paint themselves as victims. Rather than say "I made a choice that anyone could have made," and "what are the lessons I could take away for next time," they seem to want to say that they were victims of their own stupidity. They go overboard in self-criticism.

The book *Good to Great*, compiled by Jim Collins and his team, shows that great leaders of perpetually successful organizations almost always take accountability for their part in any problems with their company, but they also make immediate notes to learn from their mistakes. They also don't gloat in the successes, always acknowledging a team effort. Victims, on the other hand, feel a need to blame other people or other things for poor performance, or they repeatedly admonish themselves without learning or going forward. We will discuss this important phenomenon more in the chapter on self-esteem.

Powering through, Sailing through

Awareness of victim attitude is important and will determine your style as you go through life. As I have said before, life happens the way it has always happened since the beginning of time. Which means it is constantly changing. When we say things go wrong, what we really mean is that things don't go the way we want, expect, or plan. In truth, things happen; and you have more control over some of these things than others. But, if you have worked on your thrival skills to adapt to the new situation, you will sail through. In fact, sailing is an excellent metaphor that may help you to gain a new attitude toward the challenges in your life.

At the apex of a journey into the beautiful Arizona desert, I realized that as much as I loved the desert, I really missed the ocean. I drove straight back from Arizona to the Oregon coast, pulled up at the edge of a cliff over the ocean and bounded out of the car to gape. I'm not sure how long I sat there on that cliff meditating on the sea's constant motion. For a long time I watched the swirling, curling, breaking and changing motion of the sea, until a thought occurred to me. Life is like this. Life is very much like the sea. It has patterns like waves and tidal movements, but life, like the ocean, is constantly changing.

No sooner had I thought this when I heard and saw a noisy power boat come into my line of sight, motoring through all that swirling ocean in a straight line. I thought, *that powerboat is like my willpower*. When I want to drive events, I use my willpower like a powerboat, at least until I run out of gas. I could see that the power boat was the ultimate in speed and control, but it was also clumsy, bashing the waves loudly and ungracefully. In order to run a power boat you have to have fuel which is limited and pollutes the oceans and the air. Yet even with its negatives, the powerboat was undeniably effective. How many of us would like our life to be able to go in an easy straight line all the time, powering our way through? How many of us have met people who are like powerboats all the time and have found them noisy, bossy, difficult and inflexible?

Well, we just can't use willpower all the time, I thought. Then into my line of vision came a sailboat gracefully tacking across the ocean with its sails billowing in the wind. *Isn't this more the way my life really goes?* I rarely move toward the next thing in a straight line. I may know where I am going, but I have a series of things that I have to do first. I maneuver, I jump through hoops before I get there, or I tack (change directions) and slowly use what resources I can to get to either my original destination or somewhere else that now looks as promising or more so. And sometimes in life, like on the ocean, the wind dies and I have to wait, or at that point I can sometimes use my willpower to get things done. I realized also that in my life, like at sea, too much wind is often worse than no wind at all. We all have to weather storms, and even willpower cannot help you in a storm. You are wise to know the signs and to go into a harbor until it passes. The lessons of the sea are the same as the lessons of life.

My meditation on the cliffs that day revealed to me that whether you go with the flow in an organic fashion using the resources around you (sailing), or rely on your own willpower (power boating), to thrive means to adopt both the attitude and the skills of a good sailor. A good sailor can navigate safely and feels joy in the skills he is practicing. A good sailor knows the rhythm of the tides. He knows that winds can change. A good sailor always has a way to call for help, and won't hesitate to use it. A good sailor has invested in training, learned from others with more experience, and decked his boat with good tools and safety gear to make it secure, ready for any changes. A good sailor watches what the seas are doing and does not deviate from the habits that keep him safe on a boat. A good sailor always coils his ropes flat so no one will trip over them and so he will not have to deal with tangles in an urgent situation. Sailors are respectful of the dangers of the sea and act accordingly. This is a thriving attitude.

Are You Prepared to Set Sail?

We can learn from this metaphor to sail through life. The problem is, we rarely have any good guidance for this. We rarely prepare proactively for the possible. Consider the things that we say go wrong in life. Are you expecting to lose your job one day with little notice? I began to fully expect that I would lose my job unexpectedly, economies being what they are. That was an attitude shift that saved me from being devastated, unlike many others I saw who could not handle a major downsizing. This was very common in two critical years that affected me in recent history, after the dot-com boom crash in 2000 and after September 11th in 2001. And it continues today in these very uncertain financial times of 2009. But I survive and I thrive.

I continue to protect myself by making sure my skills remain marketable, and, in my case, are also diverse. I have learned to create my own work whenever necessary. I also know that with good habits, no matter what happens my good reputation will not go away. I will always have good references and I make an effort to keep in touch with those people. I prepare financially for the possibility that I may be out of income for an extended period. If I did not, that would be like sailing into the ocean without extra fuel, emergency flares, or a radio. Preparing for the possible is within your control. Preparing for the possible gives you license to take some risks in life. You can prepare for possible successes as well as possible pitfalls. Prepare for good weather, smooth sailing and great winds. Prepare to get to your destination sooner, or to get to a better destination than you ever dreamed. Some people have missed opportunities by not preparing for the possibility of success. Remember that a great sailing day takes the same amount of preparation as a poor sailing day. Woody Allen said, "Eighty percent of success is showing up." Prepare to sail, and then show up to sail.

A List of Things That Inevitably Happen In Life

# of times in an average life time	Type of Life Event	Examples of Real Life Events
1	Birth	Being born
innumerable	Rejection	Get rejected by schools, jobs, institutions, people
innumerable	Acceptance	Get accepted by schools, jobs, institutions, people
innumerable	Failures and losses	Get punished, lose a fight, get lost, fail a test, make a mistake, lose money, lose a job, make someone unhappy...
innumerable	Successes and wins	Tie a shoe lace, find your way, win recognition, do something solo, earn money, win a competition, make someone laugh

Often especially in teen years	Peer pressure	Take a dare, lose virginity, try marijuana, buy fad fashions, do the latest diet/exercise craze, drink too much, tell a lie
innumerable	Embarrass-ment	Walk into the wrong bathroom, put your foot in your mouth, forget a birthday or anniversary
innumerable	Mistakes	Make an error at work, make a bad judgment in car, trust someone you shouldn't have, buy a "lemon"
innumerable	Solutions	Find a product that helps, talk through and resolve a conflict, cut out what foods disagree with you...
innumerable	Pride	Master a game, sport or activity, achieve recognition or an award bestowed on you, proud of others you love
innumerable	Fear	Afraid of: the dark, public speaking, talking to others, ending your life alone, snakes, spiders, heights
innumerable	Courage	Learning something new, speaking in a new language far from home, telling someone how you feel, standing up to a bully
1 – 20 times	Live with other people	Family, roommate, lovers, partners, stay with relatives, stay with strangers
2 – 8 times	Fall in love	Fall in love
2 – 8 times	Broken heart	Break-up of a romance, death of a loved one
1 – 5 times	Make a Relationship commitment	Go steady, live together, marry...

1 – 4 times	Leave a Relationship commitment	Divorce, break-up, separation, dissolve a partnership…
10 – 200	Friendship	Gaining a friend
8 - 40	End of a friendship	Lose touch, drift apart, have falling out, death
0 – 4 times	Find faith	Find faith
0 – 4 times	Lose faith	Lose faith
0 – 4 times	Parenthood	Have children
1 – 10 times	Victim of a Crime	Burglary, assault, rape, abuse, vandalism
1 - ?	Broken the law / rules	Traffic violations, minor cheating, thievery, illegal possession, hope nothing worse
0 – 40 times	Thoughts on children	Wish you had not had children
1 - 400	More thoughts on children	Could not imagine life without children
1 – 40 times	More thoughts on children	Could not imagine life with children
0 – innumerable	Still more thoughts on children	Wish you had had children
40 - 2000	Minor Illness or injury	Getting the flu, colds, strep throat, twisted ankle
1 – 30 times	Serious Illness or Injury	Broken bones, cancer, HIV, chronic condition, serious car accident
1 – 10 times	Loss of a loved one	Death of someone close to you, a person or an animal
1 – 20 times	Get a job	Get a job, get a career
1 – 25 times	Loss of a job	Fired or laid off from a job, quit a job

2 – 8 times	Change of career paths	Fall into something new, get an opportunity, follow a passion or idea, get schooling to try a new career, try something new
3 – 35 times	Group rejection	Don't fit into any group: classroom, job, social setting, church, families, in-laws
6 – 75	Group acceptance	Fit into groups: jobs, classrooms, social groups, families, church
0 - 30	Make a major purchase	Buy car, house, expensive: jewellery, electronics, clothes, household items, etc.
innumerable	Have trouble with bureaucracy	Settling taxes, making a complaint, returning a product, fixing an error, getting what you are entitled to, waiting
innumerable	Getting stuck	In traffic, in line, in waiting rooms, in a boring job, in mental, emotional, spiritual, or physical limbo
1 – 4 times	Retirement	Retire
1	Death	Death

The above is a list of the kind of things everyone will encounter in life in one form or another. Life is diverse enough that I have likely missed a number of things; however, most people have encountered most or all of the above. This is like a sailor accepting that eventually he will run into bad weather or mechanical failures, and he also will see something special like whales or meteor showers. A good sailor has a back-up for almost everything that she may need, but also brings a camera and a journal for the special moments. But how do you really prepare for an emotional shipwreck in life? Is there a sailing attitude for that?

When Your 'Ship Hits the Rocks

When sailors of old ventured out across the seven seas without any of the weather forecasting, navigation, and communication technology we have now, storms were very real threats. There are quite a few mythologies about storms, and the earrings sailors wore. One story is that earrings were earned for traversing the two places where storms were most feared. One earring was for Cape Horn in South America and another for the Cape of Good Hope in Africa. Another story says that a sailor's earrings were a form of insurance to pay the cost of burial if he was washed ashore after a shipwreck. The simplest version is that an earring was the sign of an experienced mariner who had survived a shipwreck. Before earrings on men became fashionable, or could signify anything to do with sexual orientation, I met a man who had an earring and he told me it was because he felt that he had survived a shipwreck -- the shipwreck of his divorce.

There are few more important relationships than the one you have with a lover or a chosen life partner. I think that surviving a break-up is worth an earring, and thriving is worth more than a few doubloons. Attitudes toward a crisis in a relationship point out critical differences in the ways people either survive or thrive. What is your attitude toward separation? The thought that my partner and I may decide to separate one day is not a pleasant one, but as long as our relationship started well and has most or all of the foundations of a good relationship (in a forthcoming book I will detail the 13 elements of a good foundation for a relationship), I believe those elements won't ever truly go away. If I keep the relation-ship well maintained, the 'ship will always be afloat and stay in the water. If my relationship changes and we are not going to sail together any longer, the important foundation elements -- for example, respect -- should not disappear. That's why these elements are called the foundation. And that's why your choice of a good sailing partner is crucial.

Although it may sound pessimistic to talk about a relationship ending when I am in the midst of it, I know, if it comes to that, my current partner will be as wonderful an ex-partner as he is a partner. That is not predicting doom or being faithless. In actuality, I am speaking from a strong platform of faith in love. One of my favorite couplets from Shakespeare's Sonnet XXV is,

"Oh happy I, that love and am beloved, where I may not remove, nor be removed." Love that is true, in a strong relationship, is love that cannot be removed. My attitude is that since I have control over who comes into my life, I will choose good people and maintain good relationships.

I wish all couples, divorced or devoted, could achieve the attitude of thriving, no matter what the outcome of the relationship. Too often I see couples whose pain in going through a separation is made worse by guilt, shame and a sense of failure. Remember, experiencing pain during change is normal, and if a relationship ends even after you try to make it work, it does not mean you failed. It can mean it was a poor match, it can mean that one or both of you changed, or sometimes it means that one or both of you will need to change and now you have the opportunity. Sometimes it means you have learned to be more careful in your assessment of others. After pain, reflect on the lessons learned, and move on, knowing that it will be better next time. This is what you can do. This is what you can control.

To move forward and be kind to yourself and others may not feel like a satisfying attitude after a break-up, but it is the most beneficial and thriving attitude. Bitterness at a break-up is part of the victim mentality and becomes very damaging if prolonged.

This is the blame that does not serve. It often seems easier, if you are angry, to hate people you are leaving. Ask anyone who has tried to stop loving someone if they felt they had control over that. They don't. If you feel anger toward someone, but can't rid yourself of your love for them, you should not think of that as a bad thing. It may be a liability at the end of a relationship to still have feelings, but it should not be easy if you are a person with depth and the ability to bond. The pain is a sign of your character. Part of the problem may be that when you are missing someone you may think of them as the only love you will have. You may rationalize that if it is so strong you should not let go of the person that this love surrounds. But you can let go of the person without letting go of the love or fondness. This is wise. The attitude of letting go after trying is important. There is a point where more trying will not make it better. Imagine yourself cast adrift on a piece of wreckage and having the mirage of your 'ship, whole and perfect, in front of you. The only thing that is an error about this image is the fact that it is a mirage. Over time, when you get your feet back on the ground, when you no longer feel adrift, you can sometimes change the relation-ship into one of friend-ship. Consider that people who are widowed do not have this choice. Will the love you felt become less intense over time? Yes, it should and you want it to, so that you can feel it again with someone else or even with yourself. This is where distraction can be one of the rare positive quick fixes.   Get involved in other things that keep you from dwelling too much in the past.   You should try not to have intensity with the past when the present is the only place you can find true happiness. You do not have control over the past, but you do have control over the present.

Pick Good Crew Members and Cut the Others Some Slack

The storms you will encounter are not under your control, but your attitude will bail you out, or quickly get you landing upright on terra firma. The kind of storms I speak of will not likely be actual ones, although we know we are not immune from the hurricanes, tsunamis and natural disasters of recent times. Things will happen in life that are beyond your control: deaths, accidents, and other acts of fate. But inevitably, the storms that you will most often encounter will be those that happen in your relationships with other people, and not just your romantic relationships.

Whether it is your significant other, co-workers, friends, employers, your mechanic, other commuters in traffic, or the person serving you at lunch, people will not always do what you expect or want them to do. They may be rude or inconsiderate, say the wrong thing, steal your idea, or forget your birthday. They may break promises. They may anger you and they may disappoint you, and one day you are likely to disappoint them.

Know when to cut people slack, and know when to cut them out. Be gracious to strangers as well as to the people you interact with daily. If we make an effort to compliment people to their faces more often, we are doing ourselves and others a great service. Benjamin Franklin said "Write people's accomplishments in stone, and their faults in the sand." Be kind to yourself and be kind to others. Meanwhile, wherever possible choose friends who have proven their reliability and good friendship. Keep them close and make sure they know how much you appreciate them. Your friends will have flaws just as you do, but we are in the boat together and it's important to have a crew you trust, respect and love. If you have not been expressing your appreciation to people who deserve it, don't hesitate to verbalize it more. This may help you thrive in the way you want to, or it may not, but it will never, ever, hold you back from thriving.

In my first attempts to direct some small theater productions, I remember getting very frustrated with others. I wisely found my mentor and asked for advice. He gave me an affirmation to say to myself. Although I was not affirmation-friendly, I discovered that he was right, and what he gave me to say was an excellent reminder of the kind of attitude needed to work with others. The affirmation (always repeated twice) was "Everyone around me means well. Everyone around me means well." I have passed it on to others, especially new managers, because I know it is helpful. What is great about this affirmation is that despite what we may think, it is true. When working with others, they nearly always, if not always, mean well. It may not seem so because everyone is at the center of his or her own universe. This includes you. Others may seem inconsiderate, stubborn, frustrating, and inflexible or they may actually be that way, but they are not doing it to piss you off. You just perceive it that way. In their minds they are doing the best thing.

Being in an organization, company or family is a little like being in a boat with a crew. You cannot get away from these people, so you have to figure out how to work with them. These are rules that you can practice to make it easier.

1. Everyone around you means well. Everyone is at the center of their own universe.
2. Listen and hear what others are saying.
3. Ask questions first, shoot off your mouth later. Many shoot off their mouth first and ask questions too late. Simply reverse the order and tone down the shooting off part.

4. Do speak up! When the time is appropriate, when people are asking for your ideas, do step up and speak. People do want to know what you have to say. Start stretching your ability to take that risk if it is unfamiliar to you.

5. If you are a person who always has their own opinion and has to have your own way, then extend your ability to say yes to others and swallow your own thoughts. You may be surprised. Likewise, if you are a person who says yes far too often to others, then start trying to say no whenever you can.

6. People do not have to reciprocate your positive attitude, so don't expect them necessarily to listen – this is entitlement. You cannot be friends with everyone. You just have to get along with them as best you can. Go back to rule one.

7. When you have a chance, always try to get into situations where you can choose who you work with. If you are an experienced leader with leadership skills, step up to a position where you can lead others. In a team environment, lead by example.

8. Lighten up. Humor is invaluable to keep morale up for yourself and others.

If you can remember only rule number one, Everyone Around Me Means Well, your attitude toward others will get better. If you can add rule two, Listen, your teamwork and communication skills will get more advanced, and your own stress level will go down.

At work we can rarely choose who we work with but in personal relationships it is a tenet of thriving to choose to surround yourself with positive people.   It is also prudent to cut negative or excessively high-maintenance people out of your life. Do not do this ruthlessly, simply acknowledge to yourself that you are moving on, and let them think whatever they want to. You are just going to see a lot less of them.   Stop accepting their invitations, or accept them rarely. If you have to say something to them, think of the kindest thing to say without accusations or confrontations. Consider that sometimes we have trouble with certain others because they are revealing some of our own weaknesses, blind spots or elephants. Consider this, but while you reflect on it, see less of them.

Sailing Solo

I deliberately started off talking about relationships by talking about ending our significant ones because in order to thrive, not just survive, you do need to prepare for the possible, even if it's not pleasant. Dwelling in the rosy-ness of being in love will not show us how to thrive in relationships, because that is the easy part. Yet, losing a relationship is not something to take lightly. A person can feel beaten up and cast adrift. Like the good sailor, it is best to maintain all your 'ships, including your relation-ship with yourself if you are to thrive. But what if you are not currently in a significant romantic relationship yet? What is the attitude for sailing solo?

If you have no significant romantic relationship yet, then you can always strengthen your relationship with yourself, with others, with your career ambitions, and with your passions. Don't think of this as a booby prize, because it is anything but. The truth is, we are living this life alone as well as with others and you need to make sure that at all times you feel love and support, with or without a significant other. A strong self-love and self-support is the #1 element for thriving. If you do not have that attitude down, and most of us do not, you need to go back and work on it. Learning to sail alone gives us more strength to share when we are in relationships with others. It is also another process, and we have to understand some basics about self-esteem that are rarely taught. At the beginning of this chapter on Attitude, I started with the idea that you have to make a mental shift in attitude before anything physically manifests itself in your life. Controlling your attitude and moving toward self-awareness is a key to making sure you will move beyond survival, but it is only the beginning. We have only journeyed on to the beach of this island called the self, and in order to go further toward thriving, we are now going to venture into the forbidding jungle of the self and find out what is really going on in there. Entering into this jungle is our most important step of all. The next chapter on self-esteem is the most important chapter in this whole book.

To recap this chapter:

- ☐ You do control your attitude AND your attitude then controls you.
- ☐ You should have an attitude of awareness.
- ☐ With an attitude of awareness, you acknowledge the repeating, intermittent or chronic pain in your life. This can lead to your commitment to rid yourself of that pain.
- ☐ An attitude of awareness means looking at the elephant(s) in the living room: the big problems you are not facing.
- ☐ With an attitude of awareness, you notice your own victim mentality in all the ways you use it that are hindering you rather than helping you: blame, shame, excuses, and an unhelpful sense of entitlement.

☐ Agree to change your victim attitude by being accountable for your actions, inactions, or results, without blaming yourself or others (tricky – more on that later).

☐ Use will power only when you need to, and flow with the resources you have available. Do not expect to reach goals too quickly or in a straight, direct line.

☐ Make sure you prepare for all possibilities, especially the unpleasant possibilities.

☐ Look for growth and learning opportunities in the face of a relationship break-up and don't dwell in anger and bitterness too long.

☐ Keep good people with helpful attitudes around you, and either cut the others some slack, or cut them out of your life.

☐ Learn how to be independent and sail solo.

"I'm gonna sit right down and write myself a letter and make believe it came from you."

- Lyrics from a 1930's pop song.

Chapter Four – Self-Esteem: The Most Important Step of All

After several years of studying the ideas of success, thriving, making positive changes and being happy, I, like many others, found that it all hinges on one thing. It is what we call self-esteem, or self-love. Self-esteem is acceptance of the self. If you have full acceptance of the self, you can put this book and all other self-help books away. But most of us don't. Not even close. Self-esteem is something that theoretically, like attitude, we have total control over, and yet it is elusive and the one thing that most of us will spend a lifetime coaxing from the shadows.

It may sound hypocritical or paradoxical to say if you want to make positive, personal changes for yourself, you should start with accepting yourself as you are. This is why it took me until the fourth chapter to tell you this. If I had said this straight off, you might very understandably have closed the book. The ideas behind self-esteem are the simplest and, at the same time, the most difficult concepts of all. The lyrics from the pop song quoted at the beginning of the chapter, "I'm gonna sit right down and write myself a letter and make believe it came from you," shows the paradox of self-esteem in our society. We ourselves are capable of saying all the things we need to hear, but insist that it is only important if it comes from someone else. In our society, we feel that we need to be more than we are now. I doubt that you would have picked up this book if you did not feel this way. Likely, this book will now start departing from your expectations. I am not abandoning what I have said in previous chapters, but it is important to understand the seemingly paradoxical relationship between change and acceptance. You are still getting directions to the road to thriving, even if it looks like we may have taken an unexpected and confusing turn.

Think again of Scrooge in *A Christmas Carol*. The reason Scrooge is able to change in one night is because the spirits show him images of himself from outside himself. In effect, Scrooge is given the gift of deep understanding of what made him joyful once, and how he grew hurt and bitter. He sees what drove him forward and what held him back. He starts to remember his essential self within the miser and bitter person he has become. Kneeling on his own gravestone at the end, he accepts that he had lost himself in search of societal ideas of "success." On the grave stone, which is his own near-death experience, Scrooge must accept his true self in order to find his way back to his true self.

I once came across a photograph of myself on my 5th birthday. In the picture, all my friends were around me in their party frocks and suits. I was smiling into the camera, showing off my missing two front teeth by sticking my tongue through the gap in a goofy grin. I could see in that photograph that I was happy. When I first saw this picture again, I was in my twenties and had become introverted, living, for the most part, in fiction books. I looked at that photograph and knew that through the trauma of school and the work world, I had strayed from myself. The humor and joyousness revealed in the photo was no longer in my life. I started to try to figure out why. I saw my journey as a journey back to my essence. Later I would go into management in a company that forced me to get out of myself and discover my leadership skills. Still later, I would go to university, study theatre, and discover more of the child I had been in the photo. At a certain point, I realized, like Dorothy in Oz, my essential self (home) was not lost, but was there all the time. And like Dorothy and Scrooge, I wasn't taking a journey in which I needed to get back home, because home was always there. Now I was moving forward towards a life with greater meaning, compassion and understanding.

The compassion I gained had to start with compassion for myself. The whole reason I closed down and moved away from the happy girl was because along the way I began to believe that I wasn't good, competent, attractive or worthy of love. I was afraid of being wrong, afraid of being a failure, afraid of rejection and afraid of being hurt and humiliated. All these fears are ones that our schools, families, workplaces and our society inevitably give us while trying to prepare us for the "real" world. They "meant well." As a teacher of writing, I have heard this story many times, often pin-pointed to the exact time when we closed off parts of ourselves due to some comment that wounded us to the quick. Most of the time, others were not trying to shut us down. They were trying to help, but instead they instilled lasting fears and insecurities that we have carried with us, often since early in life.

The good news is, accepting your essential self, letting go of judgments, and moving forward is the greatest experience you will ever know. Every experience in this place of acceptance and thrival is intensely enjoyed, appreciated and true. Thriving is giving up the real world for the true world. It is learning to repeatedly give up fears and doubts for self-acceptance and self-awareness. It is giving up loneliness and misery for knowing you are never alone and you are always able to be happy. It is giving up surviving for thriving

Just Being

So, thriving is not just about "success" or moving to the next thing, or making small and large changes, or thinking about process over product. Thriving is also about acceptance and acceptance is about being. You don't always want to be doing something grand other than just living and being. In order to truly thrive and be happy many of you may need to stop feeling the anxiety to succeed. I know, you may think that if you are not successful or if you don't get off your butt and do something, you will wallow, you will flounder, you will stay stuck, you will not get the girl or the guy, you will continue to hate your job, and you will not get the things you want. Well, maybe that is true and maybe it isn't, but I guarantee that you need to create some inner strength if you want to change the dissatisfying situation you are in.

The pressure people put on themselves is often crushing and traps them in a vicious cycle of non-acceptance. Whenever you get excessively worried, or down on yourself, or down on your life, ask yourself if you are enjoying your moment right now, right here. Because that moment is your life, and you do have control over it. Whenever you dwell too much in the past, or too much in the future and are feeling uncomfortable, remember the discomfort is coming from you, not the government, not your ex, not anyone in your life. You are creating your own misery. Yet, you also own the exclusive rights and abilities to stop the misery by staying in the moment and accepting that everything is okay right now. Like Dorothy in Oz, who always had the ability to get home by clicking her heels, you too have the ability to bring yourself home.

Very few of us are actually "not okay" at any given moment. Even when someone asks us and we tell them we are "not okay," technically, most of the time we are healthy and not under any immediate threat. We say we are "not okay" because we are feeling anxiety, fear and discomfort. Experts in relaxation, stress-control and meditation say that when we feel these things, the best thing to do is to remember to breathe. When anxious, we have involuntarily put ourselves in the fight-or-flight state even if there is nothing tangible to either fight or flee from. That's when you have to override your own system with a big breath and positive self-talk such as, "I am okay" and "There is nothing wrong with me" or "it's all good" and "I'll figure it out."

Breath is the underpinning of most meditation and many spiritual practices have the aim of getting in touch with your higher self. The word *spiritual* is the combination of *spire* meaning breath, and *ritual* meaning a repeated sacred or religious practice or rite. Therefore, being spiritual can be seen as practicing a breath-ritual or life-ritual. That is why letting out a big sigh, yawn, laugh, or sneeze, especially with the vibration of sound, is an excellent and instant de-stressor. Remember Scrooge, at the end of the film, is finally able to sneeze and have someone bless him. Breath acknowledges life. A higher life is to thrive.

If you are making yourself unhappy by not accepting your essential self, you are not part of the process of thriving. I remember I used to have the horrible habit, while waiting in the cold or rain for the bus, of looking at other people at the bus stop and wishing I were anyone else but me. I would find someone at the bus stop who looked nice and imagine if I were them, how much better my life would be. In these moments of unhappiness, anxiety and lack of acceptance, we are tempted for quick fixes. All of these can be temporarily helpful to a degree. Distraction, in particular, can be helpful. But often you go right back to worrying or beating yourself up when the distraction is finished, or the experience of eating is over, or the high of the drug has worn off. So you wrongly eat more, take another hit of your drug of choice or find another distraction. If you always rely on quick fixes and distractions, the downward spiral will keep happening and you will thwart the upward spiral. This is where the discipline of not letting yourself go there is worthwhile, by practicing listening to your thoughts and allowing yourself to just be.

It requires no lessons; you simply listen to your internal or external ranting. You can ask yourself how you feel about yourself and then just listen. After listening, see how much of your thoughts are positive and how much are negative or drifting into a lack of acceptance of who you are right now. Ask yourself if what you tell yourself is something you would say to a good friend or a child. Is it reassuring? Is it comforting? Or is it feeding your fears and bad feelings? To thrive, you cannot beat up on yourself. But people too often make a habit of it and they rarely make a habit of doing the opposite. I call this *The Good China Syndrome*.

The Good China Syndrome

The Good China Syndrome, besides being a little word play on an '80s movie title, is about what we saw many of our mothers do at home. Our Moms would never pull The Good China out of the china cabinet unless it was a special occasion that they think deserved it. Likewise, most people don't bring out their good-buddy, pal-for-life, feel-good-about-yourself messages in their own heads unless there is a special occasion that they think deserves it. Stop. Stop restricting yourself to *The Good China Syndrome* and start bombarding yourself with the good stuff, now and always. Especially give yourself reassuring words during uncomfortable, painful moments when life is not easy. Be your own best buddy. You do not need to wait until you have done something special to tell yourself how great you are. And it doesn't need to come from someone else to be truthful and meaningful. It has just as much meaning and even more truth if it comes from you.

Don't worry about your ego becoming too large from all the praise and positive thoughts. That phenomenon is for people who have no awareness of themselves, but you are committed to seeing all your faults and still loving yourself. Besides, did you know that expensive bone-china plates - as delicate and pretty as they may look - have been proven in "drop" tests to be far more durable than plates made of other materials. Always give yourself the good stuff in praise, it goes a long way.

The Paradox of Shame, Blame and Change

As I pointed out, I have led us into something of a paradox. How can I tell you that you need to work toward change, and then say accept yourself as you are? This operates in the same way we experience conflict. Most people can find only two reactions to conflict and both of them involve blame. For example, two friends are in conflict over a miscommunication about a meeting place. They have shown up at the wrong place, or the wrong time, or both. One friend is irritated at having to wait and worry. The other friend is irritated at being misdirected. From each of these perspectives it is a typical first reaction to blame the other person, and think, "they screwed up," or "you're wrong and I'm right."

After figuring out the miscommunication, the second typical reaction might be to see your culpability and to blame yourself, as in "I screwed up." But, given time, people do take a third reaction of acceptance. They can acknowledge that someone else may have made an error, without blaming or shaming them. Or they can acknowledge full accountability for their own error without blaming, shaming or beating up on themselves. This is what is called the high road. We need to learn to react this way first, rather than with blame or shame. It's not easy, especially when we are programmed to direct both blame and accountability away from ourselves as a way of avoiding something unpleasant, someone else's wrath, or a justification for our own wrath.

Just as with our conflicts with friends, it is possible to accept yourself and love yourself as-is (accountability), and also to make positive changes, without making a judgment (no blaming or shaming) of who you are now. This will make the changes easier, which is why it is important for you to understand this. If making changes has been difficult for you in the past, it may be because you felt you needed to beat up on yourself to make it happen. But it is much easier to change if it is coming from the right motivation, which is not loaded with judgment. In order to get to that place, you have to create a better relationship with yourself. What is the benefit? From this place, procrastination naturally disappears. Without prodding, you will want to learn, for example, how to better organize yourself without judging yourself as disorganized, how to take better care of your health without denigrating yourself for being out of shape, how to be in control of your finances without kicking yourself for getting into debt. This is what can happen when you have a good relationship with yourself.

Most would agree that the first step to improving any relationship is improving communication. What you say to people matters and the same is true about your relationship with yourself. What you say to yourself matters.

Choose Your Language, Choose Your Life

In my home office, there was a magazine cover I ripped out and pinned over my desk. The article featured on the cover wasn't as interesting to me as the title, which was a question. The question was something I intuitively knew was important. It said, "Do words change reality?" This is an interesting question for someone who has a life-long love affair with words. It is also interesting for me because I believe the underlying fabric of life – reality – is the same for everybody. The simple answer to the question, "Do words change reality?" is: yes, words change *your* reality. In order to improve your relationship with yourself, in order to start self-acceptance and make positive changes, you are going to want to notice what pops out of your mouth. You are going to want to watch and correct yourself until you have a whole new vocabulary. Let me tell you some stories of how this showed up in my life and how it links to a person's all-important self-esteem and self-identity.

I first started to confront the words that I had been using against myself in therapy. It was my counselor who pointed out to me how much I used the word "need." She questioned whether I really needed something, or wanted it. This led to a lengthy debate on what were truly survival *needs* and what were *wants*, or the things we know will make us thrive. For example, like many others, I insisted that one of my needs was love. She insisted it was not a need. This was such a radical idea for me that it upset me immensely. I was ready to walk out of her office and never come back. It seemed obvious to me that everyone needed love. Keep in mind that what I was thinking of as love, was love from others. But she stuck to her guns and said for survival, we did not need love. There are, unfortunately, lots of examples of people who have survived without love. She was not suggesting it was a great way to live your life, or to raise children, just that it was not a need. Needs, she pointed out, suggest desperation. Despair. Who wants to live their life in despair? Yet perhaps I was living my life in despair.

At first, I resisted this idea, insisting that I certainly did have all sorts of needs. In truth, I would come to admit that I liked the drama of needing, which was also connected to my procrastination. I would let things become what I thought of as a "need," before I felt motivated to act. However, my therapist soon made me see that all I was doing was robbing myself of my own ability to choose. Later I found out that the word need is of pre-historic Germanic origin, and means more than necessity, it means distress or misery. My therapist was right: it was a word of despair.

After much work, I now say things like, "I want a vacation," replacing, "I need a vacation," or "I want to get some work done" over "I need to get some work done." I experience the power of making a choice. I no longer burden myself with a desperate, empty wish, but back up my choices with realistic actions. I make a plan to save for that vacation (process), instead of investing in lottery tickets, fantasies or blindly running up charges on a credit card (products). Those fantasy-credit-card choices deliver the promise of a product with no process. That is the thrust of what lottery tickets and credit cards advertise: fulfilling products without process. They also make products seem like routes to happiness. That is why advertising and marketing people are always talking about "creating a need." For your own life, you are going to want to know exactly where the lines are between "wants" and "needs" and watch your language as it will change your life. When I say change your life, I don't mean that it will simply change how you feel about your life, although that will happen too, but you will notice, in time, that certain fears, procrastinations and blocks will start to fall away and you will notice yourself moving forward with greater happiness. Others will notice too, and you will be treated differently.

There are other words we need to be aware of when they spring from our mouths. We rob ourselves of mental energy simply by exaggerating what we say. Do we really have a *million* things to do? Probably not, but if we believe we do, we feel weighted down. The unconscious has an uncanny knack of believing everything we tell it, including taking our bad advice. How often do you hear yourself say, "I don't even want to think about it," when mulling it over may be the first step to successful planning? Then, when we don't accomplish tasks well, we often beat ourselves up with unnecessary guilt by saying, "I should have...." or, "that was a mistake." An alternate expression of choice would be to say, "I could have... and next time I will," or "I learned from that."

Here are some Guidelines for the Power of Choice in your Language:

I need   ⇨ I want

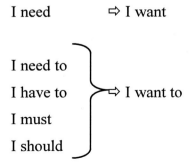

I need to
I have to   ⇨ I want to
I must
I should

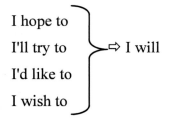

I hope to		
I'll try to	⇨	I will
I'd like to		
I wish to		

Problem   ⇨ Challenge

Mistake   ⇨ Learning opportunity

Language that does not define you but suggests a temporary state:

I am	depressed	⇨	I am going through a down period
	stupid	⇨	I did a few things I could have done better, but learned from them
	a failure	⇨	I did not achieve what I wanted to this/that time
	divorced	⇨	I went through a divorce (x years ago)and am currently single
	single	⇨	I am currently single
	unemployed	⇨	I am between jobs right now… in career transition… landing my next contract

Exercise

Write down ONE thing now that you are going to commit to watching what you say. Choose any ONE of the phrases or words above. I am asking for only ONE because changing habits takes focus and it doesn't help to splinter your focus. Once you have eliminated one negative in most of your language, you can go back and pick up another one. For now, choose only ONE that you want to keep an ear out for, and transform.

_____

_____

_____

Buddy System

I have a very good friend whom I admire named Anne, and when we hung out together we would act as monitors for each other's word choices. If we heard something very unhelpful spring out of the other's mouth, we had a shorthand comment to let each other know what we had heard. The shorthand comment, which was Anne's invention, was LSE which stood for Low Self-Esteem. So if I said something like, "I don't know what I'm doing; I'm a mess." She would inevitably respond: "LSE," and we would laugh. It gave us both an opportunity to correct what we had said.

My "I don't know what I'm doing; I'm a mess," turned into "I'm bright, I'll figure it out," to which we would also have a private chuckle of understanding.

I cannot overstate how important it is to build buddy support systems throughout your life like the one I have with Anne. Keep good company; keep positive and questioning people around you. And nurture these attributes in yourself, so you will be good company to others. Be a positive and questioning person. A person who asks you a lot of questions is helping you get clear. Sometimes it is annoying and uncomfortable as hell, but it's the kind of hell that yields you your life's work. Someone who watches your positive and negative language is invaluable. Although Anne and I do not see each other as often as we once did, we still act as sounding boards for one another. One day we talked about self-esteem again and I told her that I had turned a corner. She said, "What do you mean?" I said, "Well, I am no longer trying to address my low self-esteem. Instead I find myself asking, *what would a high self-esteem person do in this situation?*" She loved that. I said, "It often reveals a great deal about me and the gap between who I am and who I want to be."

Exercise

Write down a person or some people that you will ask to be LSE monitors for each other:

_____

_____

_____

Some people find this kind of buddy system easier than others. Often ego prevents sharing these ideas with others because in the masculine world we live in any kind of admission of weakness is frowned on. The idea behind the exercise is to make sure you are accentuating your strengths and avoiding negative thoughts that weaken your self-esteem, but it still may be difficult for some to reach out and find someone to share this exercise with. Some people will feel that they don't have a buddy they can count on, or who is around often enough. Others may be very introverted. Until you find some real-life buddies, try creating your own. I want you to imagine a buddy. You can even give him, or her, a name. While he/she is not real, they will be someone inside you who lets you know when something negative directed toward you – e.g... "I'm a mess" – slips out of your own mouth.

Loving Yourself – Can You Really Do it?

When I entitled this chapter *Self-Esteem - The Most Important Step of All*, I was entirely serious. If you don't put work in on this part, nothing from here on in will work smoothly. If you retain one thing from this book, retain the necessity to work on your self-esteem. If you think you already have high self-esteem, you should be able to answer yes to all these questions:

Self-Esteem Questions

1. Do you think you are beautiful or attractive?
2. Do you think you are competent in many things?
3. Do you enjoy time alone?
4. Do you find it easy to say "I love you" to those you are close to or have strong feelings for?
5. Do you find it easy to say "I love you" to yourself?
6. Do you think that there is nothing wrong with you?
7. When you know you have made a mistake, can you admit it publicly, and move on?
8. When you think of past failures, do you remember the valuable lessons you learned without feeling shame or embarrassment at failing?

9. Is being right or a winner less important to you than supporting solutions that work for everybody?

10. Do you have a clear sense of your purpose in life?

11. Are you known as someone who does what they say they will, and keeps their commitments?

12. Do you always give yourself positive self-talk?

13. Do you listen to what others say critically about you, but don't take it to heart because you feel you know yourself well?

14. Do you listen to what others say critically about you or your work, but don't take it to heart because you know they are talking about behaviors, and not about you as a person?

15. When you are feeling down, do you always know that it is a temporary situation?

16. Is making eye contact with others an easy thing for you to do?

17. Is talking to others easy?

18. Do you feel you have faced, overcome or reduced some major fears in your life?

19. Can you do absolutely nothing without feeling lazy?

There are few among us who can answer yes to all these questions with no reservations. The questions themselves will act as guideposts for you as your self-esteem increases. For now, I want you to focus on only one of these questions, the one that likely stuck out for you as slightly unusual. Question #5 asked if you find it easy to say "I love you" to yourself. Why is this an unusual question? Because blatant love directed at the self is one of the last taboos of our society. Money is still a touchy subject but getting less so. Death is still something people want to avoid as a subject. Once upon a time it was talking about sex that was a taboo. Thanks to a lot of great sex educators we now have no trouble talking about sex without tittering, although I find that the subject of masturbation will still get a chuckle. The other subject which is rarely talked about is the subject of happiness. If you think it isn't touchy, try asking someone you don't know that well if they are happy. Many will hesitate to say. They may well ask why you want to know. Some have described it as a loaded question. I think this is interesting and shows us the next important path that we could choose. Self-love and self-happiness are critical subjects that I do want to talk about.

I was once at a women's group in which the facilitators were conducting a brainstorming session on what people did to be loving toward themselves. Several pampering suggestions were given, like relaxing in the bathtub, making time for one's self, or reading. These were all met with nods and sounds of agreement, but when one woman said masturbation, the whole group broke out in laughter. As it turns out the woman who suggested this was a sex therapist and the facilitator, in her wisdom, praised her suggestion. But our spontaneous reaction of laughter interested me. Although we can think of sex as love-making, we are not taught to think of masturbation as an act of self-love. Sex nowadays is boldly bragged about, but masturbation is still thought of as juvenile and is not talked about. Woody Allen has a great comeback line in his movie *Annie Hall* when Diane Keaton is trying to shame him about masturbation he says, "Don't knock masturbation; it's sex with someone I love." When people are not in a loving partnership, some will increase their masturbation, and some will not, but very few will consider it an act of self-love rather than a consolation prize. Most think of masturbation as a release or a way to "get off." Few will use masturbation as a nice loving thing to do for one's self in combination with loving thoughts directed toward the self. I recommend anyone not in relationship – or even if they are - to start looking at both self touch and masturbation in a new way and stop thinking of it as a consolation prize.

In your life, which of the following happens more frequently? Telling someone you love them, or being told by someone else that they love you? Imagine which event has brought up greater feelings of discomfort, fear, wanting to escape, or utter vulnerability. Is it when someone is telling you they love you, or when you are telling them that you love them, or perhaps both? If one is more uncomfortable for you than the other, it can indicate whether you tend to be more of a giver or a receiver. I started to notice that it was easier for me to say "I love you" than to hear it. I realized my concept of being in love was to be crazy about someone. But, if I thought someone was crazy about me, I would also think that perhaps they really were crazy. Anyone who was madly in love with me had to be desperate, right? This is LSE. You need to learn how to receive love as well as give it. Both are important, and if you have LSE you may need to work on either of these and explore why you have trouble with one or the other.

As I said before Question #5 is unusual because it asks you if you can easily say "I love you " to yourself. This is a bit of a ruse since most of us have never, ever, said "I love you" to ourselves at all, let alone said it easily. The closest people get, is to say "I like myself" or "I love myself" which is not quite the same thing. I have found in working with this subject that it is quite powerful to say "I love you" to yourself and learn how to give to yourself, and receive that which you want. Directed at the self, the "I" and "you" in this phrase are seemingly the same person but psychologically the "you" is accepting, and the "I" is giving. They identify themselves as distinct. Therefore, to say "I love you" to yourself is a gift changing hands, rather than just a statement of fact like "I love myself." In this form it becomes a powerful, simple to remember affirmation that you can direct at yourself in any situation.

You will likely not want to say it out loud. You will simply want to say it to yourself internally, but I have already discovered that even though others can't hear it, people have a huge amount of resistance to saying "I love you" to themselves. They think it is weird or they don't believe it is true, and so they are indescribably uncomfortable with it. And the same people who resist this idea often have no trouble saying horrible and hateful things aloud to themselves, even the words "I hate myself." We too often find out that we are committed to self-hate, and not committed enough to self-love. Believe it or not, this small thing, this self-love talk is something that will help you conquer fears and contribute to your happiness as you go through the challenges and achievements of life. Self-love is essential for thriving.

The other self-loving talk that I encourage people to say to themselves to raise their self-esteem is "I forgive you." If you offend someone and ask them to forgive you, remember also to forgive yourself. A character on the popular late '90s TV show *Ally McBeal*, Richard Fish, used to say "bygones," immediately forgiving himself any time he might have offended someone, which was frequently. The character of Fish may not have been able to tell others he was sorry, but he was always able to move forward happily by saying "bygones", despite challenges, failures, and judgments against him. Fish always landed on his feet.

Exercise

Okay, you know what is coming. Try saying "I love you" to yourself before bed every night. The beauty of this exercise is that you don't have to share it with others. Even if you have a partner in bed next to you, who is telling you that they love you, remember this exercise is about self-love. This exercise will help you more easily love and accept others, and also be able to accept love from others more easily. Even Scrooge, at the end of the film version of *A Christmas Carol* is able to accept a kiss from his nephew's wife and a "Bless you" without saying "Humbug."

As well as being a good daily practice, this exercise can also help you get you through a stressful situation, a moment of fear, or a time when you feel lonely. If you make this into a habit, in many cases something interesting will happen. Just as negative thoughts sometimes pop into your head unbidden, at times you may find that the words "I love you" will also pop into your head as if from someone else. Some will say this is a message from God or your higher power, but regardless of what you believe, it will have a powerful positive effect on you. To get started you have to meet this love half-way by giving it away. I had a wise acting teacher who used to say to her students, "To give it away is to keep it." I don't think any of us really knew what she meant, but it stuck in my head and it applies perfectly in this situation. Give it up for yourself and it will stay with you.

The other exercise you can practice is to forgive yourself immediately rather than beating yourself up immediately. Start including "I forgive you" into your self-loving vocabulary.

Do not under-estimate the power of self-love. As I have said, the higher your self-esteem grows, the more your fears and procrastinations will disappear.

To recap this chapter:

- ☐ Just be. Take pressure off yourself and just be yourself.
- ☐ Don't hesitate to praise yourself – Avoid the "Good China Syndrome."
- ☐ When "mistakes" are made, be accountable when appropriate, without shaming or blaming yourself or others.

- Be aware of what pops out of your mouth and give yourself language with choices - language without blame or shame.
- Use a buddy system to make sure you are aware of LSE language.
- Practice saying loving things to yourself, including "I love you."
- Periodically review your self esteem questionnaire to see how you are doing.
- Start thinking, what would a person with high self esteem do in this situation?

Chapter Five – What Matters

Worrying in the Present about the Past

When I was 19, I was getting ulcers from worrying so much. My shoulders were a mountain of tension at the end of a day. Slowly I started to dissect what was bothering me. Usually they were small things, but I had taken them to heart instead of letting them go. Someone had beeped their horn at me in traffic, I made a mistake at work, or I received an unexpected bill in the mail. All these things made me feel bad about myself and my life. Because it was affecting me physically I knew that I had to choose. Rather than die young I would have to let go of these irritations of life. I decided to ask myself this question: Was this something that I would care about, or even remember, in five years from now? The answer inevitably was no. I would likely not care five years from now if someone had snapped at me, or if I had made an error, or if someone had honked their horn at me in traffic. And if it wasn't going to matter at all to my future, I would not let it matter now. I recommend this technique for you worriers, who spend too much time in either the immediate past or the immediate future. Go through all your worries and ask yourself the Five Year Question. Then, when you have diminished your worries, start practicing staying in the moment. Stay present, feel what you are feeling, let it wash over you and be gone. The now is the moment that matters.

If there are things that the Five Year Question doesn't dispel, then try this adjustment. Look at any of the accomplishments you have made in your life that you feel went well. We all have at least a few if not numerous things. Ask yourself if you could have predicted five years before making that accomplishment, that it would happen. Note that you can rarely predict the road to an accomplishment in the future. Because of that, there is no sense worrying about what will happen right now. Sticking to what you are doing in the moment, or to a small goal, will bring you through every time. These techniques give you in-the-moment control over your fears and anxieties. That way, you develop a sense of what matters and how to avoid losing energy to things like worry. Staying present in the moment, or using that worry energy to act and accomplish small goals, will reward you now, and move you toward thriving.

My own methods may or may not work for you. Here is the story of a good friend of mine and how he dealt with his worries and obsession with the past. Some people have a more complex way of dealing with worry and also emotions like anger. Here is a touching account from my friend Barry about how he creatively stopped worrying and obsessing.

Once in a while I do something daft that really embarrasses me. Usually it's because I let myself be overwhelmed by anger about somebody at work or in my personal life. I bottle it up for months or years and then blam! I've learned to apologize and that's fine if it's something small, like criticizing the newspaper delivery guy in the middle of a snowstorm because he threw the paper from the sidewalk and it slammed against my front door, when I hadn't bothered shoveling my front walk.

But when I act like a big-time bozo, I brood for months afterwards. I remember all the other times in my life when I've screwed up. At a certain point I realize that this thinking is actually taking up a lot of time.. Instead of relaxing I pace the floor, reviewing my sins and imagining revenge. Back and forth between blaming myself and blaming others.

Four years ago I stumbled on a way of fighting back. I went to a psychologist who encouraged me to describe a time when I really embarrassed myself and a time when I was particularly proud of myself. For the stupid occasion I remembered when I got seriously hurt playing basketball by being reckless and really scared my friends and family. For the proud occasion I remembered a time when I had, in the space of a year, moved from being in lousy physical shape to being in great shape.

After several sessions with the psychologist, I figured out what to do with these two memories. I had recently seen the film Crouching Tiger, Hidden Dragon. I devised a tale that began with me lying under the blanket beside the basketball court where I got injured. Under the blanket with me were gremlins representing all the times I'd made an ass of myself. Suddenly I found myself flying up into a tall tree beside the court like a Chinese warrior. Far below me I could see the gremlins scuffling about under the blanket, making noises like Alvin and the Chipmunks, pissed off because I had abandoned them.

Then I imagined I was flying up the valley o a hillside. My hiking buddy says to me: "Hey, you're doing pretty well." We climb higher. "You've been working out!" he says as I lead him up a steep slope. As we stand on top, he stares at me: "Man, you're back!"

We hike down to a pond below the peak, layer up and relax. As we eat lunch, the humiliations of the past are far away.

I told myself this fable for a while, and soon I stopped obsessing about the past and got on with the present. I wonder why this worked so well. I think one element is lightness in several dimensions. Self-criticism in the extreme is so heavy and doomful. There's a pleasing sense in my becoming a superhero, side by side with the image of distancing myself from the embarrassing past.

Anger, Emotions, The Hole Inside, and What Matters

Notice that Barry said he had a problem getting rid of anger and wasted a lot of time "imagining revenge." Anger can be both positive and negative. It can be a powerful motivator to positive change. Imagine if Gandhi, or any other people we think of as great emancipators, never became angry? The trouble is, anger can be one of the emotions that makes you feel as if you are doing something for yourself, or even others, when you are doing the opposite. Most people are not directing their anger positively, or choosing their battles, or directing their energy toward positive results. Some people walk around pissed off and sucking their own positive energy away. Most of us are guilty at times of overreacting to small irritants when we could get better results. Many people could learn to let go of anger if they could realize that the people suffering most from their wrath are themselves.

Directed outward with no thought or wisdom behind it, anger frequently comes back to bite you. If you are in the anger and revenge mode frequently, ask yourself how it is serving your life right now? People notice and sense people who are angry or are carrying around repressed anger, and will try to avoid them. They frequently do not open up to them, and they do not share information with them. If you are a person with anger, could you be sabotaging yourself from making good connections and not even know it?

Put simply, in our ongoing search for self-fulfillment, many, if not all of us, have a hole inside that we are trying to fill. The hole is where the self-support and self-esteem is weak. This is where fears and insecurities and doubts hang out. Our quick fixes are ways we try to fill this hole with whatever makes us instantly feel better: food, alcohol, TV, drugs, anger. There are positive things to fill this place with too: self-love, humour, good company, artistic expression, exercise. The positive fillers yield optimistic, longer lasting results for the mind, body and soul and keep one on an upward spiral. But, as with negative quick fixes, we have to keep replenishing the supply. Anger is a tricky and powerful emotion that can be protective or destructive, or both. The question is: are you using your anger towards what matters? As you go through the limited amount of time you have on the planet, you may want to think about how you are using this powerful motivating emotion. Have you grown in your development of anger? Children act out and react to situations with anger because they do not think about what matters in the long run. They have not developed a sense of control. They have not thought things through. Even as adults many of us need to develop control over this emotion rather than indulge in it.

I also went through an angry-young-woman stage in my twenties and thirties when, instead of worrying about everything, I wanted to fight about everything. I seemed to have a penchant for conflict and rebellion. Which was fine, and sometimes worthwhile, as it did motivate me to start doing some terrific things, but not always.

I can put it in perspective now, as mature people do. Less and less do I want to indulge in anger. I recognize that anger often misdirects my energy into things that don't matter, and destroys things that do matter, like my peace of mind, my relationship with myself, or my relationship with others. If someone or something arouses my anger, I ask myself: do I really want to ruin my day by taking on someone who baits me, or can I let it go? Can I control how it may escalate? Sometimes I have to bounce these questions off of someone I respect, my boss, my friend, my partner, to come up with the solution. We all need someone sensible to vent to. These people can help you answer the questions of what you may want to let go of, by understanding what is worth fighting for – choosing your battles, or choosing to change what you can change and is worth changing. People, for example, are something you can't change. You can ask them to change, but you cannot make them change. Remember the people I mentioned who were put on probation at work, but who ultimately were not able to change? To know that you cannot change others takes maturity and wisdom. To know that you can change yourself and your reactions takes more of the same.

I am not telling you never to argue or work on things you want to fight for, because you can change people's minds with compelling arguments, but you can't change who they are or how they act, without their own decision to do so. On a one-to-one basis, telling people how you sincerely feel is more effective than trying to police them. Do you want to waste time and energy trying to make a change happen with anger alone? Is it worthwhile to your energy level, or stress level to fight? This comes down to your beliefs and values, what matters to you, and your own habits, as well as a clear understanding of what you can't change.

I have watched people spend money, time, and energy on law suits to fight the government or each other, and the only people benefiting in the end are the lawyers. And even many lawyers find it stressful to deal with these ugly issues. I have watched people break into reactive fights and suffer consequences later. Even after the consequences, which should have told them in hindsight this was not a worthwhile fight, they frequently get stuck in blame, and ignore the lesson. They rarely want to reflect on a better way for them to act, or not act, which would have yielded better results. People don't like to do things the best ways; they prefer the easy way with immediate satisfaction – quick fixes. Anger fixes are potent and a prime reason that some people stay stuck in survival. Whether you express it or repress it (like Barry once did), learning to let go of things that do not ultimately matter is learning how to thrive.

If anger is an elephant issue for you, you may want to start by reading about this subject. There are also many excellent courses in Conflict Resolution and Anger Management that can give you active exercises for practice. There are also excellent coaches and counselors versed in this issue. Invest in these so that you are not wasting energy on old survival tactics, instead of moving towards terrific thrival tactics.

Small Changes are Small Miracles

I have talked about elephants but often what matters most are very small things. Although many people discount these things, they can make a world of difference in your life. I wrote a comedy play for radio entitled *Small Miracles*. In the play a man discovers a store in which small miracles are sold, the price of which is doing good deeds. When shown the small miracles for sale, he thinks they are rather silly and worthless. They include such things as: the bus will be late when you are also late, the Friday noon-hour line up at the bank is light, next time you lock your keys in the car, you will also leave a window open, etc. The man decides that he can live without these small miracles in his life. As you might predict, his decision comes back to haunt him. He misses a bus that is critical to help him, he gets stuck in a line-up at the bank and he gets his keys locked in his car, all at critical times when he desperately needs to attend to other things that can keep his career, marriage and life together.   By the end of the story he starts to wise up and sees how these "small miracles" that he creates with a good attitude, the good deeds, really do make his life go much smoother.

While this radio play was a comedy and not meant to have a hugely serious message, the idea that small things contribute to our success is very true. Unlike the story in the play, there is no place to buy a miracle and there are always things that we cannot control, but like the play the small changes we can control and choose to implement, do have a profound effect. The Zen teacher and author Cheri Huber says the way we do anything is the way we do everything. This may seem extreme but let me give you some examples of how small changes or habits do eventually turn into those small miracles.

In the *Putting Off Procrastination* course that I teach, there is a project assignment. At the end of the course, after an assessment to give each person some self-awareness, and several exercises, I ask each student to create one small, better habit in their life. These are some of the small changes students chose to make their small miracles:

- [ ] To put my keys in the same place so I stop searching for them
- [ ] To stop saying the word "need" when I mean "want"
- [ ] To start saying "no" to some of my friends and co-workers requests of me
- [ ] To always make a note of where I met someone on the back of their business card and file it in a business card file so I can find them again.
- [ ] To hire someone once a month to do some of the housework that I never get to
- [ ] To set up a filing system and use it
- [ ] To throw flyers and papers away into a recycle bin instead of hanging on to them "just in case" and to take recycling away to pick-up bins as soon as it is full.
- [ ] To make my bed daily
- [ ] To stop buying so many things at Dollar stores and consider buying quality things that I can use for life

The effect of these small changes is much larger than one can see on the surface. Several of these small changes, which take anywhere from three weeks to six months to make into life-long habits, will save these people precious time in their lives. For example, the person who searches for their keys daily, trying to remember where they may have put them down, is repeatedly wasting three minutes or more a day looking. At the end of a year that can be over 18 hours of wasted time. That is more than a day's waking hours lost. Consider that this person has been allowing this bad habit to continue for several years and you see that they have lost several days of their life doing something that annoys them, stresses them and wastes their time.

If networking, sales or business connections are important to what you do, then setting up a filing system or making notes on the back of business cards assures that you make important connections, and also has similar effects in saving time. Small changes can be very important to the one currency that can equalize all our lives: time.

The other decisions people made involved saving space, like making the bed daily, buying fewer cheap and frivolous items, or recycling paper clutter promptly. Not only are the effects of making a bed or reducing clutter aesthetically more pleasing, but people found they had places to sit down, that there were less surfaces covered so that they could work without losing things and other benefits. It is also documented that clutter can be a symptom or a contributing factor to mental diseases. It does not surprise me that the first tenet of the Chinese discipline of Feng Shui, which is about attracting positive energy by use of space, is to rid your space of clutter. Curiously enough, Feng Shui originates from the

I Ching or the Chinese Book of Changes. The ancients knew that small changes and habits affect their lives profoundly.

But what is perhaps far more important is that all of the small choices people made have a big effect on their self-esteem and ability to feel that they have successfully managed something. Often they reap the rewards of these habits by seeing the fruits of their change in front of them every day. The accomplishment, albeit appearing small to others, reminds them that they are capable of improving their lives successively and successfully. So, the way they accomplish these things is the way they will accomplish, by ingrained memory, all other things, or as Huber says, "The way we do anything is the way we do everything."

What can you accomplish? I used to tell people if you can pull off a dinner party you can accomplish event planning. I had a group of friends who used to make a game of one-up-man-ship in dinner parties. Thanks to them I knew the nuts and bolts of putting on a good to great dinner party. But until I was the General Manager of a mid-sized non-profit arts organization, I had never pulled off a very large project under very short time lines.

Our artistic director envisioned and researched a wonderful theatre, dance and music extravaganza, designed to raise funds to help stop the tide of teenage suicides. However, this event had numerous unique obstacles and challenges. At one point our mega-shopping mall venue wanted to back out. We had to figure out how to legally and safely fly a teen performer down a 100-foot drop on a wire. We had to actually make custom seats – rentals were not possible - that didn't overwhelm the cost of the production. And, we had to figure out how to market the show to our target teen audience which was suspicious of anything made by adults. I had hired a great team, but none of us had ever done any of these things before and the team was looking to me as their leader. As the General Manager, I was the person ultimately responsible for seeing that everything was accomplished.

The whole time, I kept thinking: this is just like a big dinner party that you plan with someone else. You have to consider logistics (when and how to issue the invites, when and how to pick up the groceries, when to start cooking, etc.), acquisitions (where to get budget decorations, food, and entertainment), delegation (who will pick up the food, or bring extra chairs), calling in favors (who has a recipe you can use, who will lend you their cookware, who will help in the kitchen), attendance (who to invite, how to invite them, what should the RSVP date be, who is finalized to come), and budget (how can I do all this without shelling out a small mint). I knew that if I could put on a good dinner party -- and I already knew that I could do that -- then I could make this show a success. Even under the short time lines, all things were taken care of one by one. Everything was brainstormed, delegated and planned. When things did not work out, we adjusted the plan to make it work. We maintained good working relationships despite tussles and disagreements.

As it turned out, we packed every show with the teens we were trying to get through to, and many came back for more than one show. When we received not one, but a number of letters from teens saying that the show had made them reconsider suicide and get help, the gratification was priceless. Although the accomplishment was not mine alone -- not by a long shot -- I knew that I was able to pull off my role with poise and self-assurance by keeping my dinner party mentality. On some level, I understood that how you do anything is how you do everything. By using the dinner party, an event that did not intimidate me, as a metaphor I was able to accomplish something on a much larger scale with excellent results.

Your values

In addition to giving proper credence to very small successes and
how they influence your life, it is important to understand the value
system which motivates you. If you feel an ethical conflict with
anything you are doing, you will be suffering internally or you will
sabotage what you are doing.   As an example, remember the
employees who are on probation, who can't seem to change
although their manager wants them to?   I often saw that beneath
these scenarios was simply a clash in values. The manager has a
"work ethic" value. The employee has a "make work fun" value.
The manager is a "shut up and put up" person and the employee is
a "communication is key" person.   The manager has a
"conventional thinking" value and the employee has a "creative
solutions" value. As you can see neither of these people are wrong
or bad, they are just not operating from the same value base.
Ultimately, the manager has to have the right mix of people on her
or his team who have complementary values and skills to complete
their daily goals. Likewise, the employee or employees have to be
in a situation where they can use their strengths, and be in sync
with others ways of operating.

It is always interesting to see exactly how out of whack a company
gets when the market changes, or larger forces demand that the

whole organization make changes. The values and competencies of the founders or senior managers which initially invited success, sometimes become a hindrance. They hire people who understand the new direction the company needs to go in, who have the competencies and values to accomplish it, but inevitably they are in a constant battle with the very people who hired them. I have seen this on more than one occasion. Sometimes it happens in only one or two departments but often it permeates throughout an entire organization.

The good news is that in your personal life you have much more control over managing change than a company does. You are the founder, the entrepreneur, the department manager and the employee all rolled into one. The bad news is, it can mean that your priorities will have to change to get what you want. Most people will not want to change their value system, although it is possible and sometimes can be beneficial. What most people want is to find a place where their values and strengths can thrive. This will involve a process of evaluating yourself, and the best way to do that is to look at what you are currently doing in your life and what you are currently prioritizing in your life.

Exercise

First let us start with a general idea of what is important to you. Prioritize or rank the following things into what matters most for you. What comes first in your life, what comes second, etc.

Health _____

Your significant love relationship _____

Friendships _____

Children (your own) _____

Family (the one you grew up in) _____

Career, Work, Business, Money or Art if you are a career artist_____

Ask one or two people close to you, who know you well, if they can see in your *actions* these priorities. What we are looking for is that your priorities are not just wishful thinking. We want to see what you have done and are doing towards these things. They may reveal that the priorities you profess are different from those that you are exhibiting.

Next, I want you to take these different areas that I define as health, and prioritize them as well:

Health – mental _____

(reading, dialogue with others, and what affects your self-esteem)

Health – body _____

(anything that effects your physical health)

Health – soul _____

(your spiritual or artistic practices)

Health – financial _____

(investments for future)

Next, what are your core values? Choose (circle) one value from
each column for a total of five. Try to stay within the columns but,
if necessary, break the rules and take more than one from one
column.

Personal Growth	Positive Attitude	Wisdom	Communica-tion	Education, learning
Practicality	Change	Teamwork	Health (well-being)	Faith, spirituality
Love	Creativity	Freedom	Variety	Adventure
Concern for others	Home	Challenge	Joy	Family
Achieveme nt	Fun	Money, wealth	Persistence	Power
Self-Reliance	Status	Discipline	Strength	Hard Work
Truth	Results-Oriented	Risk (willing to take)	Accounta-bility	Competitio n Loyalty
Resource-fulness	Commitment	Reliability	Integrity	Trust
Democracy	Country, patriotism	Honesty	Law and Order	Tradition
Security	Fairness, Justice	Peace	Diversity	Non-violence
Community Equality	Unity	Tolerance	Gratitude	Selflessness
	Generosity	Friendship	Simplicity	

Yes, it's hard to choose only five but this is only an exercise and it
is not carved in stone. Now, think about how you live your life
now, what you say to others and how you show others that you
stand by those words. Fill in the blank table, following the
example.

Example:

Value	What you DO to show that Value	What you SAY to show Value
1) **Health** (well-being)	Work out and play sports regularly Eat well and watch my diet	"Health is number one."
2) **Community**	I participate in my church community, and sit on committees and boards. I live in a community within walking distance of friends and where I know many business-owners and services.	"Community is why I live where I do."

3) Friendship	I make a point of having a lot of social events for friends and keep in touch with them frequently.	"I am a good friend. My friends are important to me."
4) Self-reliance	I try not to be in debt to anybody unless for a good reason/investment. I can help others better if I am more self-reliant.	"Don't go thinking the world owes you anything, it was here first."
5) Home	Have created a cozy sanctuary for a home.	"Home is where I find peace."

If you are not currently doing anything that reflects something you think of as a core value, ask yourself if you want to start doing something. Or, do you want to change that value to one you are doing something towards already. If you are unsure, I recommend the latter for now. You may want to get a buddy to look over what you have chosen and see if they agree that those are the top values you express in your life.

Value	What you DO to show that Value	What you SAY to show that Value

Remember these choices above are your beliefs, not what is necessarily true, but it is important to start to think of these beliefs as critical influences on what you may adopt as your values. This may be totally acceptable to you or it may need some growth.

There may be some beliefs or expectations that you feel are holding you back and that you may no longer want to abide by.

All of these exercises are for self awareness. The priorities are your priorities and you may decide to re-order them by the time you finish this book. For now, what you have done is clarified what matters to you now. By becoming aware you may simply embrace the clarity or you may choose to make some changes and put things in alignment.

Alignment

If you become more aware of your values, you may also want to check that they are in alignment with your priorities.

1. What you BELIEVE or VALUE needs to be in alignment with what you DO
2. What you DO needs to be in alignment with what you SAY
3. How you stay healthy while accomplishing all this needs to be BALANCED in your health plan.

Like all success, getting things into alignment is a successive process and does not happen overnight. For one thing, we often pursue false values, thinking that they are real. Scrooge, as you may recall, chose in his life to change his values and harden his heart after he was hurt. When he changes at the end of his night with the spirits, he is really returning to the true values that he used to have. When he was younger, he once admired his gracious and affable employer, Mr. Fezziwig, but because he chose to repress what was a core value and replace it with the pursuit of money, he himself became a cold and unmerciful employer. This is when he started moving from thriving to surviving despite his accumulating wealth.

Most people will have no trouble grasping the idea that what they believe, and what they do and say, should be in alignment. You are probably now looking at what you wrote down and searching for anything that is not in alignment. That is good. However, I recommend that you do not try to fix it or do anything about it immediately. I especially don't want you to feel bad if you find something out of alignment. All the exercise requires is your awareness. It means moving things from the unconscious to the conscious. You will change it in a natural flow after appropriate reflection time and as you decide to act on changes you want to make in your life. That said, balancing your health plan will take a more proactive and immediate effort on your part. This is where you might want to expend some energy and thought. In fact, I decided that it was so important that it deserves its own chapter.

To recap this chapter:

- ☐ Use the "5 Year Rule" and any other techniques to stop unnecessary worrying.

- ☐ Be aware of what you use to fill the hole inside, be it addiction to emotions or other things; introduce positive fillers: humor, self-love, exercise, etc.

- ☐ Small changes can often make the largest differences, and give you instant success (successive progress). Small things can often show you how to do larger things. Are you being self defeating by trying to go too big always?

- ☐ Discover how your words and actions reveal your real values – are they what you expected or want?

- ☐ Bring some awareness to aligning your values with your words and actions.

Chapter Six – Your Health Plan

If You Haven't Got Your Health

When you hear "health plan" you generally think of health insurance or a benefit that you or your employer pay premiums toward. This is all very good, but one of the errors of North American thinking is that health is something to which they are reactive and not proactive. In other words, you pay attention to your health only when there is a problem with it. Your health, especially after you become an adult and as you progress, is something that I believe should be far more preventative in nature, regardless of whether it is good or not. The other mistake we make is thinking that health is all about the body, when physical health is only one aspect of health, when for me it comprises one of the four pillars.

The four pillars are mind, body, soul and finances. The last one, finances, you may think has been filed in the wrong category, but if you think about it, it is difficult and stressful if you are unable to financially take care of your family's health or your own health, especially as you age. Financial health is as critical a component to your health in this world as schools are to education. In certain traditions and cultures people understand this without thinking about it. Even in the symbology of Tarot cards, which have ancient origins, the suit of the disks or pentangles represents both physical health and financial health. The disks can be symbols for food as well as coins or money.

The other health categories of mind, body and soul, with the possible exception of soul, are, for the most part, understood by most people as things that contribute to your health. When I realized how critical my health was to my well being I made an agreement with myself that I would never scrimp on money in that one area of my life. I will often justify paying for things because I know it is for my health. In addition to committing to spending more money, I choose to devote more time to health as well. To thrive you will want to be very actively involved in health matters on a daily and weekly basis. If you are not, I can nearly guarantee you that you will eventually be in some kind of pain that you do not need to be in, as well as many other consequences.

Health for Your Mind

In looking at mental health I am going to ask us to look at old Scrooge again. At the beginning of Dickens' story we see that Scrooge will not engage others in dialogue, but avoids people, suspecting they want to take something from him. When Scrooge is visited by men on a charity drive who try to engage him in a dialogue of compassion, he shuts them out dismissing them with "Are there no workhouses? Are there no prisons?" Scrooge sticks to what his own set opinions are and does not try to expand his mind. His mental capacity for dialogue is restricted, he is alone, and he shows all the signs of a recluse.

Since Alzheimer's runs in my family, particularly in the women, I am particularly sensitive to mental health. My mother had Alzheimer's and my grandmother had Alzheimer's. In my grandmother's day it was not called Alzheimer's and very little was understood about this dementia. More recent long-term studies have revealed that people who keep mentally challenged by reading and having daily dialogues with others are far less likely to contract Alzheimer's as they age. Also, daily exercise and general activities is another attribute of those who are far less likely to get Alzheimer's or other dementia.

My grandmother was in her sixties when it was noticed. She was not a reader and had no formal education. Also, she had been separated from daily contact with my grandfather who had to be hospitalized in his sixties so even though she visited him often, she lost some of the important daily contact she had with her partner. In contrast, my mother was in her seventies before the disease was noticed. Though my mother was a big reader and had a Master's Degree in Education, she was very introverted and reclusive. My parents had been divorced twenty years previously and unlike my father, my mother never remarried or even tried to date. She did get involved politically and was very close to her sister. I think that it was her reading and involvement with others that helped her to resist the disease longer than my grandmother. Unfortunately, despite numerous encouragements from her children she became more and more reclusive and did not go out as she got older. It was then that we noticed the first signs and eventually had to put her in a home for 24-hour supervision. In the home, we found she got somewhat better and certainly happier because she was forced to interact with others. Unfortunately, Alzheimer's is a degenerative disease and once it has taken hold will eventually take over. It also effects the body as much as it effects the mind, as the brain controls all other motor functions, so people often think dementia and Alzheimer's is about mental health when really it is about both physical and mental..

The studies on Alzheimer's do tell us a lot about mental stimulation and interaction with others being key to one's long-term mental health. Even diversions like playing games with others, or having hobbies that stimulate the mind and body, or are interactive with others will help enormously to keep a person in mental health. Most people who are dealing with a family member with mental health issues will note that many different mental illnesses include the tendency to be reclusive. There are studies suggesting that greater human interaction does help prevent some mental health conditions.

Some researchers suggest that recovering from mental illness is easiest in India, not because it has great facilities or science, but because of the attitude of people there. Whether they take their loved one with mental issues to a guru, shaman or a Western medicine doctor, they literally surround the patient with family support, interacting with them daily. Mother Teresa once observed that North Americans suffer from a greater poverty than India because they suffer from loneliness. Unfortunately, for some people the shyness and loneliness is something they never overcome, but just get used to.

In another study from Northwestern University in Chicago involving 2,000 men over a 30-year period found that men who showed evidence of social avoidance– (shyness) were 40 percent more likely to die from heart disease. Now it may be argued that these things are physiology and that we can do nothing about that, but we also know that we can change our own psychology and physiology with effort. I suggest that any tendency to withdraw, or avoid daily interaction with others should be fought within all of us, even if it is our natural inclination to be introverted, and yes there are also studies that suggest extroverts, or people who have learned to be more outgoing, do have better overall mental health and a better chance for thriving life skills.

Another aspect of good mental health is the mental interaction that literacy can give. In the 1980s The World Health Organization recognized that in order for adults and children to be mentally healthy they need to nurture a strong inner life, and that can be developed through literacy. Learning, and also writing of any kind gives our minds a work-out. This literally keeps the folded lobes of the brain tight. This means that the synapses where electrons fire stay connected and we are able to make thought connections. Mental health is much like physical health, if you feed your brain challenges and interaction, it is like exercising a muscle; it will physically keep in shape and in tone. In degenerative mental diseases the folds of the brain's cortex start to separate and the synapses become disconnected.

Other mental diseases can be linked to chemical imbalances which we still know little about but can be linked, in part, to the foods we eat and what we ingest which affect our serotonin levels – the feeling of well being hormone. The amino acid in foods known as tryptophan is one such serotonin level affecter. The physical stimulation of exercise can also increase serotonin and increase the production of other hormones which help give us an elevated level of happiness and well-being.

What you feed your brain in ideas and thoughts also has an effect on your health. What you read, and who you talk to, can make a big difference. People who have tendencies toward paranoia often seek out the reading material and the companionship of people who reinforce paranoid reactions or conspiracies based on sketchy and controversial information. People who have a tendency to blur the lines of reality, will often seek out magical texts, psychics or other sources and can let their interest become an obsession and can even get delusional. This can have some dangerous implications. I am not trying to bash New Age or age-old ideas, as many are beneficial. Nor am I a non-believer that there are more things in heaven and earth than are dreamt of in anyone's philosophy, as Shakespeare eluded to. Unfortunately, there are many people who, through their unhappiness and their denial, become desperate, want to feel special, and fall victim to charlatans, scam artists or well intentioned but ineffective practitioners.

A healthy dose of skepticism is just that, healthy. We seem to have forgotten that there was once an age of true-to-life snake-oil salesman, but in this day and age there are even more out there who profess magical and miraculous things and tell you all you have to do is believe. Instead, try giving yourself a balance of ideas and seek out counterpoints. Closed-mindedness in any one direction can produce tunnel vision. After all, part of us wants to believe or imagine that Scrooge did in fact meet the Spirits of Christmas. We are happy that Dickens' creativity imagined it as possible. Our imagination of unlimited possibilities makes us see solutions that help us thrive, and we should never be ready to close that down. Sometimes it is difficult to see where we need to be open-minded and where we need to be grounded, but knowing the difference is one of the tricks of thriving. If you have trouble knowing what you should believe or what to do next, it will help to seek assistance of professionals.

Enlist the Professionals

It is absolutely necessary from time-to-time for all of us to enlist the services of professionals to sort out obstacles and challenges, to face fears, to tackle grief or malaise, to restore balance and to help get us more clearly on our path in life. It may also be crucial to help us build self-esteem. Whether it is a consultant, a coach, a psychotherapist, a counselor, a doctor or other health professional, the professionals are there for a reason. While it is important to have friends to lean on, use as sounding boards and ask advice from, they do not fill the role of a trained professional. There are a number of reasons for this. One reason is the obvious; the professionals are trained, and hopefully, experienced. A professional helps build self-esteem by being positive with their clients, asking questions, and letting the client figure out the solutions. Friends, God bless them, will often want to be a little too direct in what they think about you and what you should do. Another reason is that professionals can be more objective, since they do not have a history with you. A friend may be blocked from seeing your potential just because they only know you in certain contexts. And probably one of the most important overlooked reasons is that a professional relationship, unlike a friendship, is not a reciprocal relationship. A professional is there for you and you alone. You do not have to listen to their problems. The focus and attention is strictly on you and more work can be done for you in this relationship than in a friendship. If you know you are a "care-taker" or "fixer" type of person, it is especially important for your therapy that you can neither take care of nor fix the person across from you, such as in a professional relationship. For many, the intimate sharing in this relationship, without fear of abandonment or abuse, demonstrates a healthy respectful relationship, which may be needed. With a coach as a guide, a client may gain a greater sense of their own proactive power and be able to focus on changes that will move them forward. The upshot of this is that if you have never considered going to a professional for support, you may want to reconsider it for the great many benefits.

Many people fear that if they start with a professional they are going to be seeing them for a long time before they are "cured" or have their difficulties worked out. In truth, on average you should only need to see a professional 3 to 6 months at most, and after that you should fly solo and return only if necessary. Some people only resort to counseling in a crisis, this tends to be men, others go to the professionals to help them get more out of their life, and this tends to be women. In coaching, however, men feel it is acceptable and even a sign of status to have a personal coach. They also like that coaches do not dwell on the past but focus on the future. While it may be essential as well as advisable to get professional help when you are in a crisis, don't wait for that to happen to consider a professional. All you have to want is some guidance.

If you feel you can't afford a therapist check if your company, or the company where your spouse or another family member works has what is called an EAP (Employee Assistance Program) or an EFAP (Employee and Family Assistance Program). These programs have qualified counselors for use by employees and usually their family members as well. They can help either by phone or in person at no charge. Most universities and some colleges also have free counselors. There are government agencies that can provide professional counseling sessions or peer counseling. Virtually all church pastors, ministers and temple leaders provide counseling to their congregations and often have training to do so. You can also ask your family doctor for solutions. Some private counselors have sliding scales for rates. Good counselors and coaches will often do a first session for free so that you can decide if this is a good match and you can also negotiate the fees, or terms of payment. For coaches, you may want to get a referral and also ask about sliding scales. A good search on the internet can often yield great results. Some coaches are willing to barter coaching services for a desirable service that you are able to provide for them, i.e.: bookkeeping, physical training, or whatever your trade may be.

If you decide you need a coach, counselor or other professional, I have some suggestions for success in making a good choice.

1) Go into the session with one of your elephant-in-the-livingroom issues in mind, or find another issue that you want to tackle right away. You need to focus your therapist and take responsibility for keeping them on track. Just make sure that it is truly a key issue for you. We usually have blind spots about the things we would benefit from changing first. When in doubt, you can ask a trusted friend if you think you should do some work on _____. If they respond with a hearty "yes," you may indeed have an elephant. But even if you don't have a definite focus, the therapist may find something behind your issue. Go with it, especially if it either makes you go Aha! or makes you angry. Either can help you.

2) Choose someone with some training and certification that you understand, and who acts wholly professionally. This usually means they explain what they do and don't do, and they can tell you about their training. Be wary of counselors with only one or two courses or programs. Be wary of counselors who work out of their home. Be wary of New Age counselors. Though some of these may be good, there are many charlatans out there. Also, take friend's referrals with a grain of salt and do your own research.

3) Choose professionals who make you do proactive assignments. If your counselor, coach or therapist never makes you do any assignments to get you thinking, exploring, reading

or actively reflecting, then you could be spinning your wheels in a very expensive way.

4) Coaches and counselors will specialize in certain areas so find one who has a specialization in the subject you want to work on. Try to find one who has read the same books you have read on the subject. Yes, that does mean that you should try to do some reading and research on the subject before showing up to a session. You may find that all you need is the reading. But to find out if you and your professional are on the same wave-length ask up front what books she or he has researched and if he or she is familiar with the same ones you are. My most successful collaboration was with a therapist who started as a complete stranger. No one had referred him. I found him after I had e-mailed several local therapists whose e-mail addresses I had got through a professional association web site. In the e-mail, I asked them if they were familiar with a particular book on my elephant subject. I wanted someone who was familiar with both the subject and the ideas that were explored in this one particular book. Out of 15 counselors, only one replied that they were familiar with the book and had used it in their therapy. That was the right one.

Other Ideas That Won't Cost You a Bundle

The other possibilities for inexpensive help are support groups which you can also find via the internet. They can be 12-step groups or other kinds of groups. A Toastmasters Club can boost your confidence, communication and leadership skills as well as help you overcome any fears of public speaking. If you can conceive it, no doubt someone else has put people together around it, either on-line or in face-to-face meetings. Some associations and agencies will do referrals to peer support groups. You could even start you own around a book. I know of several groups that sprang up around Julia Cameron's book, *The Artist's Way*. The point is, lack of money is no excuse. There are many possibilities for helping you get clear that do not cost a lot of money. The pursuit is always worth it.

As I taught creative writing for a number of years to adults, I always encouraged them to keep a journal. I told them there were no rules. You did not have to write in it daily. It did not have to be "good" writing. It did not have to be deep. I don't know how many reluctant students I persuaded to start a journal but I think it probably totaled up to a sizeable number over the years. Occasionally I would run into an ex-student and they would inevitably thank me for making them start a journal and tell me about how it had helped their lives. If nothing else, a journal can be a constant best friend and the cheapest of therapists. I buy inexpensive journals and stopped counting how many I went through after I had about eighty of them. If I ever want to reflect on my life or celebrate how I have progressed I dig out an old journal and start reading. The insights are well worth it.

Any of these suggestions can lead you towards strengthening your mental-emotional health. Try writing a journal; try hiring a professional; try reading more; try joining a club or group. While any one practice may not be the whole solution, it will contribute to expanding your mental horizons, making you more self-aware and moving you toward happiness, which can be the cornerstone of your Health Plan for Your Mind. If you have any doubts that successfully thriving individuals use professionals and support groups to help them get to thriving, do a little research on the people who you admire. Most people who are truly thriving have either read or written extensively, found mentors, or have used all kinds of training, associations, schools, churches, ensembles, management groups, leadership groups, clubs, therapists or other professionals to support them. No one does things in isolation from others.

Health for Your Body

The trouble with Western philosophy is that we separate mind, body and soul. I am also guilty of this. I have, however, already made some cross-overs by mentioning that diet and exercise affect your mental and emotional health. I will say up front that I am not any kind of expert on the human body. But I will say that *you* are the only expert about *your* body. Any health practitioner who tries to tell you they know more about *your* body than you do, please remind yourself that they are only a consultant. You are the only one who has known your body your whole life, lives in your body now, and will ever after. You are the expert. Only you can be the one to know what practices will eventually make your body feel healthier and happier and progressing you towards optimum health.

One of the main challenges in discussing body health is doing it without associating it with body image. Body image is, again, a self-esteem issue and for many in this culture an extremely contentious one. The painful judgments we put on our own bodies are mortifying. For too many of us the phrase "the grass is always greener in someone else's life" seems to go double for someone else's body. The best I can offer, at this point, is to stop thinking in terms of your ideal body size, shape or features and instead repeatedly go back to optimum health possible for your body. *Focus on this and only this.* In considering your Health Plan for Your Body, if your mind strays to anything else other than optimal health possible, you have to put it back on the loving track of giving yourself the gift of a healthy body.

In the body, many memories reside, including much pain and happiness. While you may take much more intense therapy to let go of intense body memories that are painful, what I want to tell you is how to feed your body for happiness in the future. When I say feed your body, there are five kinds of nutrients:

1. Food
2. Movement
3. Rest and sleep
4. Breath or air
5. Sex

For an optimally healthy and happy body you will want to keep all five in balance on a regular basis. If you are more out of touch with your body than you would like to be, it may be a challenge to balance all five of the above health aspects for the body. I suggest you choose ONE area to focus on and get better at it. Move on to the others later. The one I recommend for most people to start with is the big one for most of North Americans: food.

Food

It may seem obvious to say that food is one of the things your body needs to be healthy and happy, but what I mean by happy and healthy is optimum health with optimum enjoyment. Some people have a love-hate relationship with food. Some people have what I would say is a soulful relationship with food and are into cooking and cuisine. But very few of us will not have some kind of passion for some kind of food.

To help you understand how you may think about food, I want you to visualize what it would be like to have $500 to either stock your kitchen with any food you want or go out for meals until the $500 runs out. Which alternative would you choose? Where would you go to dinner? Somewhere where portions are larger? Somewhere that is pricey and artistic? What kind of cultural food background would you choose? What kind of variety? Now, take a moment to close your eyes and imagine a kitchen stocked with all your favorite foods and see how it feels for you? Do you already do this, or do you never do this? What foods do you usually choose? Would you take some risks since someone else is paying, or buy the same things as usual?

Take what comes up for you in this exercise and reflect on your own relationship with food. What describes it best? Choose more than one if you need to and add your own descriptors.

Exercise on Food

Your Relationship with Food:

- ☐ Is it sensible?
- ☐ Is it healthy?
- ☐ Is it indulgent?
- ☐ Is it conflicting?
- ☐ Is it tempting?
- ☐ Is it scary?
- ☐ Is it a reward system?
- ☐ Is it depriving?
- ☐ Is it balanced?
- ☐ Is it greedy?
- ☐ Is it about comforting yourself more than feeding yourself?
- ☐ Is it simply a necessity that sustains you?
- ☐ Is it soulful?
- ☐ Does it bounce around between several of these things? If so, which ones?
- ☐ Other: _____
- ☐ Other: _____
- ☐ Other: _____

If your attitude about food does bounce around, what do you want your relationship with food to be most of the time? Think of someone you know well who you feel has a happy and healthy relationship with food. What is it about their attitude toward food that you like?

I believe eating food is a happy experience. I believe that eating un-healthy food is also a happy experience, but with unhappy results. The unhappy result can be excess fat, lethargy, indigestion, skin problems, malnutrition, and other health problems, some quite serious. These problems can lead to further unhappiness which some of us counteract by eating more because, as I said, eating is a happy experience. Unfortunately because the results do not happen immediately we don't associate eating unhealthy foods with unhappiness. Imagine if every time you ate something unhealthy, you were to immediately experience pain, or a bitter taste, and no pleasure. We may stop eating unhealthy altogether. We might have no health problems, but that is not our reality. The reality is eating is pleasurable whether it is healthy or unhealthy foods, and often more pleasurable with unhealthy foods. But, if we were to only eat the healthy foods, we would have no occasional indulgences that make our banquet rich. Unfortunately, once again we have to be our own keepers.

The good news is, eating healthy foods is also a happy experience. And, on the whole, if you are eating more healthy foods it is going to be better for you. Reduced to the simplest form: quality in equals quality out. Quality-in is keeping your weight balanced and your body fed with the best nutrients. Quality-in is energy increasing. Quality-in should give you smooth, untroubled digestion. If you do have indigestion from foods you would not suspect of being unhealthy, you may have food intolerances and need to eliminate or reduce certain things from your diet. Quality-in means your skin gets smooth, soft, attractive and blemish-free. Quality-in means reducing your risk of future health problems and potentially eliminating any health problems you currently have. Quality-in means happiness. Quality-in means, well, well worth it.

What I want you to do is to find foods that are both quality foods and happy foods for you. This means you are not going to look at the price tags. My mother comes from Scottish heritage and by George she liked to save money on food. While lots of the foods we ate were healthy and cheap, there were just as many happy-healthy foods that we never ate because they were considered too expensive. I had to retrain my Scottish buying habits to buy the healthiest, high-quality things that I really enjoyed eating and not the cheapest, lower-quality things to eat. Even our Mr. Scrooge, who could well afford quality foods, is depicted at the beginning of the film version as suffering without extra bread rather than spending more money. Later he is able to thrive by chowing down at his nephews and feeding the whole Cratchit clan by giving them a prize turkey. If you spend money on good food and share good food, you will never miss the money and many believe it will always come back to you. It does, in the form of good health and good relations. It is the epitome of thriving.

Everyone is different, and food for optimum health will be different for everyone. It will be different for different bodies, different ages, different sexes and for different lifestyles. Do yourself a favor and read health articles or books on nutrition and diet. It can be any books. You do not have to commit to any one philosophy or idea and certainly I am not suggesting that you go on a diet! For now, just gather information. Each book or article will tell you something you should know about this amazing thing that we put into our bodies everyday. If you feel ready to move on to action you may want to get some advice from a nutritionist, dietician or naturopathic doctor on what foods fit your body. You may want to join a support group as well like Weight Watchers, Bulimic and Anorexia Help Groups, or Over-Eaters Anonymous. If you have serious health concerns or a history of food allergies you should see your naturopathic doctor or medical doctor for diet advice, although GPs traditionally don't know a lot about diet, he or she may be able to tell you what foods to avoid for your condition, may give you an appropriate check-up, and wants to know when you are trying new things. If you have been accused of having an eating disorder that is a serious issue that needs trained professionals to help you.

Another Exercise on Food

I want you to make a list of happy-healthy foods for you. I have started a list of my own happy-healthy foods to get you started. You may want to try eating more of some of these foods, or add unfamiliar ones to your diet. At the end of the list add some new ones and try interviewing some friends or co-workers and ask them what their happy but healthy foods are. When you finish the list, choose about ten, and start including more of them in your diet.

- ☐ Asparagus
- ☐ Apples
- ☐ Almonds (Raw)
- ☐ Steamed Broccoli
- ☐ Stir-fried veggies
- ☐ High cocoa content Chocolate bars (75% or more)– in small amounts

- ☐ Lite coconut milk in cooking
- ☐ Sushi – California rolls and other maki and nigiri sushi with seaweed or omega rich fish
- ☐ Japanese Gomae - spinach salad with sesame sauce
- ☐ Pomegranate juice found in the health food store
- ☐ Vanilla soy milk or plain soy milk
- ☐ Shrimp
- ☐ Onions and Garlic in cooking
- ☐ Crab
- ☐ Scallops
- ☐ Salmon or fish of your choice
- ☐ Seaweed rice crackers
- ☐ Curried rice
- ☐ Wild rice
- ☐ Chicken soup, home made, with plenty of spices garlic and veggies (but low salt)
- ☐ Good quality honey
- ☐ Spanikopita – spinach pie
- ☐ Hot water and sliced lemon with honey
- ☐ Feta cheese – if it is genuine goat cheese
- ☐ Romaine lettuce
- ☐ Bottled spring water or filtered water
- ☐ Tofu in all its forms and products

☐ Extra Virgin Olive Oil (& balsamic vinegar) to dip bread in (in replacement of margarine or butter) or to use on salads.

☐ Salsa (salsa with olive oil makes an excellent yummy and healthy salad dressing)

☐ Your Own: _____

☐ Your Own: _____

☐ Your Own: _____

☐ Your Own: _____

☐ Your Friend's: _____

☐ Your Friend's: _____

☐ Your Friend's: _____

☐ Your Friend's: _____

Now choose ONE thing from the next list that you will agree to say goodbye to and, if you are feeling up to it, four others that you will reduce your intake of:

☐ Regular or Diet Pop or any other sugary or aspartame drinks of any kind (Frappachinos and Starbuck's like coffee drinks too!)

☐ Deep fried foods of any kind (tempura too)

☐ Beef

☐ Pork

☐   Alcohol

☐   Breads, pastries, muffins, pancakes and bagels (unless with whole grains or non-wheat flour)

☐   Cheese or milk (soy milk is okay)

☐   Sugar in coffee or tea

☐   Candy and Jello or anything that is almost all sugar, like hot chocolate mixes

☐   Margarine, Lard or Butter

☐   High saturated fat content foods (check labels or ask for nutritional info). 4% or less saturated fat content, or a maximum of 5 grams of total fat (saturated and unsaturated) per 100 grams are guideline targets.

That's it. That's how small the list is of foods most North Americans ingest far too much of. I was shocked to learn that all that "healthy" orange juice I guzzled would not only kill a diabetic but was the same thing that professional body builders would use to add fat quickly to their bodies when they had reduced too far.

You don't have to ever give up anything forever, but if you can say a big goodbye to one of them (sugary drinks were my goodbyes) and start to reduce a few of the others on a regular basis, you will increase your health and longevity and reduce your chances of chronic or even fatal health problems. Good luck. Take it slow.

It's a process. You can't do it all right away. You will go up and down, but eventually, if you keep returning to the effort, you can get it. You may find that when you revisit these lists in a year or two that you have started eliminating or reducing many of these things unconsciously. That's right. No effort, other than awareness.

Sleep

If you did not know these before, here are some facts about sleep:

- ▶ Most North Americans are sleep deprived and frequently get under 7 hours of sleep a night.
- ▶ Over 100 million Americans and Canadians experience some form of insomnia
- ▶ Having regular adequate sleep, the good old solid eight hours (sometimes a little more, or a little less for some individuals), is one of the most crucial factors of keeping our immune systems strong, counteracting the effects of stress and making it easier to throw off milder viruses like colds and flu, or battle more serious immune deficiency viruses.
- ▶ Studies say sleep disorders or deprivation can be associated with or significantly exacerbate the following conditions: asthma, cancer, diabetes,

epilepsy, fibromyalgia, acid reflux, multiple sclerosis, complications with pregnancy or longer labor, SAD, suicide and sleep apnea.

▸ Sleep expert, Dr. Daniel F. Kripke, after being involved in numerous studies, says that all sleeping pills, including newer varieties on the market, have varying and sometimes very serious side effects and frequently are not a viable long term solution to insomnia. Also, over-the-counter products to help people sleep do not improve daytime performance. In other words, drugged sleep is not any better than a short sleep.[v]

▸ According to National Sleep Foundation, too few doctors ask their patients about sleep when assessing health.

▸ British Airways and Research International surveyed 1,000 professionals during National Sleep Awareness Week® and found that 25% admit to falling asleep in a meeting due to sleep deprivation and 70% felt they were less productive after traveling.

▸ A federal study conservatively estimated that each year over 100,000 police-reported motor vehicle crashes are caused by the drowsiness or fatigue of the operator and 1,550 deaths and 71,000 injuries are the direct result of a driver falling asleep at the wheel of a motor vehicle.[vi]

The research abounds on the negative effects, usually from lack of sleep, or in some cases, too much sleep, and how it adversely affects our health. It is a significant, but frequently overlooked, factor in the health of our mind, body and soul. We need to sleep naturally, we need to dream, and we also need to rest when our body tells us to rest.

I would love to be able to convince employers in Northern climes that employees should be on reduced work hours during the winter flu months. Allowing employees to sleep in an hour more or indulge in flex time as strategy to reduce sick days would work far better than flu shots. But, even though there is evidence to suggest more sleep, washing hands more frequently and a few other precautions could do just that, we often overextend ourselves when we are most vulnerable.

Tips for Sleeping

- No caffeine after noon. Avoid alcohol for nightcaps too, as it inhibits deep restful sleep.
- Exercise during the day. The body thrives from exercise and will rest better with it too as long as it is not done just before bed.
- Don't worry about falling asleep. The great Catch 22 of insomnia is that if you worry about getting sleep, it keeps you

awake. Simply assume that you may be awake all night and, in the meantime, try these other ideas for dozing off.

- Go to your "safe, cozy place," in your mind--if you don't have one, design one. Through my spontaneous probing of people's sleeping habits I discovered that a number of women in particular, including myself, have a cave (very womb-like), that they "go to" before falling asleep. Mine is very warm, dry, with a fire and lots of furs to sleep under, (to heck with politically correct animal rights thinking, this is my fantasy!), cozily tucked-in and protected from the wintry elements outside.

- Avoid light sources and make your room as dark as possible. Turn off all your lights, get heavier curtains, and do not succumb to the temptation to stare into light sources like TVs or computers right before bed. Light throws off your circadian rhythms. The age of electric lights was the era when the modern insomniac was born. All lighted dials or switches in your room should be shut off, covered with heavy tape, or turned to the wall, especially your lighted clock displays or dials.

- Invest in a better bed. You spend a third of your life there and it affects the other two thirds, so make sure you have a comfortable, slightly firmer bed and the right pillows (not necessarily expensive ones) and try the techniques of a pillow under your knees or between your knees if back discomfort is a sleeping problem.

- If you are a late-night worry wart, you can try jotting in a journal with the idea of diffusing your worries.

- Another mind technique is to imagine a switch that has two settings, "will" and "whim." When you are awake you are enforcing your will, so switch the switch from "will" to "whim". Now imagine two dials that are marked "observer" and "initiator." In your mind, set the "observer" dial up to a maximum setting and "initiator" down to its lowest setting, zero. Having done this, try to observe your thoughts rather than initiate them, and make sure you are thinking in a whimsical way and not invoking your will power to organize your thoughts. Sometimes you have to go back and re-switch and re-dial a few times before your controller mind lets go.

If every one of these techniques fails, then there is only one thing to do--go with it. Relax. Enjoy. Phone an insomniac friend, go to a late night cafe, scrub some mildew, or raid the fridge. Try to avoid the TV, but otherwise, do whatever turns you on, but don't punish yourself for being out of sync with the rest of the world. Be sleepless, but happy. Revel! You're not alone. You're an insomniac. Be proud.

Rest

Is resting as important as sleep? To my mind, yes. These days our frenetic 24/7 rapid-transit pace is exhausting. There are so many possibilities put before us it is no wonder most of us camp out in front of the TV for an average of 6 hours a night, even when we know it isn't healthy or restful and has an addictive quality. Our nine-to-five clock-watcher mentality insists that we try to be active and alert for a minimum of 7.5 hours of the day. We are fooling ourselves. I am not suggesting loafing but I am suggesting we pay attention to our natural rhythms and find or create as much balance as possible in your work day. Going out for a walk around the block can be restful. If you are always eating lunch at your desk, and I know we are all guilty, try having an indulgent lunch away from the office at least some of the days of your week. Weekends should not be all about resting so that you can tolerate another work week. This is not thriving.

I find women to be at particular odds with the modern world in this respect. Women have a natural monthly cycle and a waxing and waning of energy levels. But we push ourselves, or even use drugs to meet our many commitments rather than plan a slow-down, or surrender to our natural impulse to rest.

Proper rest needs to be distinguished from couch potato habits. Rest should be balanced with healthy eating and snacking to maintain your energy levels throughout the day, and the need to hydrate regularly. You need to rest when your body tells you it needs rest. Some will need a change of scene and a light walk. Others will do something that rests them, such as reading for pleasure, doing a puzzle, giving themselves a foot massage, meditating, socializing, stretching, staring out the window, yawning, etc. One thing you must not do is feel guilty for taking rest moments, because we need them. Without them we are less productive in the long run and we certainly won't thrive or enjoy life as it happens.

Movement

As with food, I believe movement for your body should make you happy. I am not a huge fan of gyms. Although some people love them, I think the word "work-out" says it all for me. I knew a woman who came from France and she said that there were two things she noticed about North Americans that contrasted sharply with the French. First, she saw that North Americans drank far too many sugary drinks. The French only drink water or wine, and because of this they are much thinner and live much longer. The other thing she could not understand was why we were crazy about gyms. In France, any activity or recreation has to be something you enjoy doing. They play football (soccer), ride bicycles, dance and do any other activity that is truly joyful to them. For myself, there are very few things that I truly enjoy doing at the gym to move my body. I decided to get happy like the French, and do the activities that I love to do rather than just what I need to do. To be honest some of these activities were things I had to learn because I had never tried them before, like rollerblading, which always looked fun to me. This took some courage. Later on, my partner convinced me to move from "just dancing" into swing dancing lessons. Both of these things I enjoy thoroughly. I don't feel like I am exercising or doing what I "should" do. Whatever moves your body cannot be bad as long as you don't overdo it, or under do it. You are the expert.

The antithesis of work-outs is what I call fun-outs. Fun-outs are different from work-outs in one principal respect; they appeal to the child in you. Let's face it, even if you love your yoga class, it probably appeals to the adult in you. Try to think of what appeals to the child in you, what connects to joy and that *Oh goodie!* feeling. This may be something adventurous, like parachuting, or it may be a game you have been playing since you were a kid, like hockey. It may be gardening because the child in you loved to play in the garden and help your Mum and Dad. Or it may be fly fishing because you used to live near a creek where you grew up, or ballet because you have always admired ballet dancers but were never allowed to go to lessons. Fun-outs cover a wide gamut and it is up to you to figure out what they are and make sure you have them in your life. At the end of this chapter there is an exercise that will help you do this.

In any physical activity you will want to acknowledge your limitations. Despite what the child in you wants, your adult body may not be advised to try somersaults or cartwheels anymore. If in doubt, consult your doctor or a fitness expert. As much as I want to encourage fun-outs, the adult has to intervene and do what is good for you and your adult body. I heartily recommend work-outs as well as fun-outs on a regular basis, even if it is doing ten-minute stretches at the office, or step exercises in front of the TV. Make sure you give your body both joy and discipline. If both are engrained in the body, you are blessed.

Playing a musical instrument can be very physical and can count as your activity, as can swinging on a swing set or riding a teeter-totter with your kids. Try things. Feed your body with movement that is 100% fun and intriguing to you. Sign up for something that you always wanted to try. Go for Tai Chi, line dancing, clowning or horseback riding. Eventually you will work up to taking that fencing class you've always wanted to try (I tried rapier fencing for the first time at age 44). If you try it and love it, you will figure out how to afford it (and often others will help) because it will give you energy and make you thrive.

Exercise on Exercise

Below, I want you to write down your **two or more** weekly fun-outs and your one or more standard weekly work-outs:

Example for those who prefer <u>Moderate</u> exercise

> **Fun-outs:**
>
> Choir (Tuesday)
>
> Walking and talking group (Sunday)
>
> **Work-outs:**
>
> Stretch and strength class (Monday)
>
> Yoga (Wednesday)

Example for those that prefer <u>High</u> exercise

> **Fun-outs:**
>
> Cycling (three times a week in good weather)
>
> Fencing (Saturday)
>
> Dance lessons and dancing (Monday)

Work-outs:

Weights and gym routine (Thursday)

Exercise bike inside in poor weather

Example for those that prefer <u>Low</u> exercise

Fun-outs:

Aqua-fit (Mondays and Thursdays)

Work-outs:

10 minutes stretching a day in office, and other in-between

moments

Your turn:

Fun-outs: **Work-outs:**

_____   _____

_____   _____

_____   _____

_____   _____

A footnote to this, if you finished your sailing, clowning or horseback riding course and you either do not want to continue, or cannot continue on a regular basis, start sniffing around for something new to replace it. Some of us thrive on variety, others love routine. Some of us have irregular work schedules or are on the road frequently so it is a challenge, but not impossible. I know of travelers who will quickly find the salsa dance places in every town and drop-in, with their dance shoes.

Health for Your Soul

When you are down to your last few dollars, spend half on bread and the other half on flowers.

- Chinese Proverb

"Life is a banquet, and most poor suckers are starving."

- Auntie Mame
(from the Oscar-nominated movie, *Auntie Mame,* 1958)

Auntie Mame was trying to say that life is rich, yet most of us dwell on what we don't have. We see only our poverties, and not how incredibly rich life is. We are starving our souls. The Chinese proverb above is saying something else about our riches. If you cannot feed your soul as well as your body you will not thrive.

All things that feed your mind and body can also feed your soul, but to thrive each person must make an effort to seek out soulfulness and beauty. Auntie Mame was right, life is a banquet. While a banquet takes work to prepare, the greatest banquets are labors of love. Soulful things awaken the senses immediately. If you are not including these, and staying awake to their powers on a daily basis, you are not nurturing thrival. The nice thing is, all you need to do is stay awake to it.

There are five mortal senses and also what has been called a sixth sense. I don't mean the sixth sense as in spooky movie terms but I do mean a sense beyond the physical senses. The word ecstatic which often described a powerful religious bliss means "out of body" and "out of mind" but not in the crazy sense. It doesn't mean being out of your senses, it means being beyond your senses. Many mystical religions and other philosophies try to induce a nirvana-like state through various means. Some use meditation and breath-ritual. Others use chanting, trance, prayer and incense. Some use dance and some use poetry. To my writing students I would define the paradoxical role of the poet. A poet's task is to use words to go beyond words. Poetry enlightens in a way that cannot be explained in a linear manner. You either get the poetic "Aha!" or you do not. In the same way, ecstasy is achieved using the senses to go beyond the senses.

I am not suggesting you need to reach ecstasy however, awakening your senses is a way to get nearer to your soul and soulfulness. In everyday life, reawakening your senses and noticing the banquet of riches around you should be part of your Health Plan.

Do you admit that you may be guilty of not fully appreciating the banquet of everyday life?

☐ Yes, I admit it, I sometimes forget how rich life is and get caught up in "making something of myself," instead of enjoying the banquet.

Even in the movie, our Mr. Scrooge finds the delight in his new ecstatic, soulful practices. After his evening with the spirits -- which is an ecstatic experience because he watches himself from outside himself -- he finds he wants to indulge in all sorts of soulful practices. The first thing he wants to try on Christmas day is to stand on his head, to the distress of his housekeeper, and he is thoroughly delighted by the boy in the street who he asks to fetch him a prize turkey. He pulls a practical joke on Bob Cratchit and laughs out loud. Near the very end of the classic movie version, Scrooge admits that he has been wrong, and engages his nephew's wife in a vigorous waltz around the room. Scrooge is allowing himself to enjoy the banquet that is life.

Julia Cameron, in her book *The Artist's Way,* suggests you should make "artist dates" to see great art, be it movies, paintings, sculpture or literature. I agree that this is a great way to bring art and inspiration into your life. Artistic expression of any kind is a direct connection to the soul. Whether you are a spectator or the artist, including culture and art in your life will help you to thrive. I am not talking about Shakespeare or jazz here. There are just as many things that are not see in galleries, theaters, concert halls or opera houses. It can be home cooking, fabric arts, decorating, comic books, collecting antiques, public speaking, hats, photography, pottery or computer graphics. Any artistic expression is soulful if it has a culture, holds ideas and strives for quality, grace, beauty or pleasure. In other words, collecting beanie babies may not make the list (or maybe some would argue it does), but many other things decidedly do.

If you have a creative bent to express yourself, or you are an artist, you owe it to yourself to explore your art or interest. Take the course you have been promising yourself. Get involved in it. Many people I know struggle with balancing their artistic passions with their careers, jobs or work. After investigating it, and being on the journey myself, I have come to the conclusion there is no one way. Everyone has a different story. I know that many have made sacrifices for their art and many others have made mental shifts to encompass different ideas of success. Even more people have found that they can do well at business or make money at a career while having an artistic life that is richly satisfying and feeds their soul. Some artists drop out of the business of success to be artists again, and to reconnect with what drew them to their art in the first place. Many Hollywood actors go back to the theater. Many musicians stop trying to make it big, or continue to be on top, because it is destroying the joy of making music for them. They prefer to get back to Health for their Soul, Art for their Soul.

In my first position as a manager, many years ago now, I used to go out at my lunch break and spend five to ten dollars to get a big bunch of flowers at a corner market across the street. Five to ten dollars bought quite a few flowers in those days. I would take the flowers into a back room where there was a sink and tell my staff not to bother me for twenty minutes as I blissfully arranged flowers in a big vase. When I was finished, I put the vase out where all could enjoy it. Many men and women in other departments would walk by and comment on how nice the flowers looked and throughout the week we all had the soulful joy of looking at those flowers. This was a great way for me to de-stress, and to share something non-work-related and soulful with my co-workers and staff. True, I could have bought already arranged flowers but the process of choosing them and putting them together was a therapeutic, artistic and joyful process that appealed to my senses. It also touched that sixth sense by going beyond my senses and making myself and others feel good in an immediate and experiential way.

I can also say that a change of scene is good for the soul. My flower arranging helped me bring nature into the urban environment of the workplace, but sometimes it is really helpful to change your scene. Nature, in particular, is replenishing to those of us who are dedicated urbanites. I remember after a particularly stressful work period lasting several months, I took a weekend trip to Vancouver Island and we went walking on one of the stony beaches, skipping pebbles, watching eagles, feeling the surf, counting jelly fish and discovering the unbelievable creatures found in tide pools. Although I am careful to keep my stress managed while I am at work and make sure I exercise, keep my sense of humour and do what is healthy, nothing could top the soulfulness of that afternoon at the beach. I felt greater stress relief and replenishment than anything I had been doing, because the environment I was in was so completely different and so divorced from office time.

That said, it need not be nature that replenishes your soul but just a change of environment. Have you been stalling on a trip away?

Are you a country person who needs a trip into the big city to see a concert or the latest movies?   Or have you neglected seeing someone you haven't seen for along time?   Getting yourself out of your normal context is what your soul sometimes craves.   The soul needs to empty itself of the routines that we have crammed into it for days on end.   This is one of the reasons we call them vacations which comes from the word   "vacant," meaning "empty."   You have to empty yourself before you can fill up again.   Although I was regularly walking and rollerblading in the park, my soul needed more than this kind of "nature" because it had also become routine.   What my soul needed was to be completely outside anything familiar.   Again, soul craves ecstasy.

Health for Your Pocket Book

Money knowledge is not evil.   It is an important skill that too many of us go into denial about.   I used to be one of those people who thought that if I put a parking ticket in my glove compartment it would magically disappear.   I was worse when it came to saving, but we will go into details of money and your relationship with it in the next Chapter on Money and Me.   It is necessary now to acknowledge that your financial relationship is a health issue.   One of the reasons that I consider it a health issue is, like it or not, it does have a great impact our ability to take care of ourselves.

Each State health department commonly collects statistics to create a report on the mental and physical health of its citizens. Among the information collected is the correlation of income to number of sick days taken in a year. In 2001 the income level that tended to have the best health overall was the annual $50,000 to $74,000 USD range. Health tends to marginally improve with greater income, but does definitely decline with less income. When income drops below $35,000 annual salary, numbers of days of sickness start to increase. Now this may be a chicken-or-egg statistic. Does poor health contribute to income loss? Or the other way around? I do not believe income establishes health, especially as I define it. However we cannot deny that as we age, health costs, even in Canada with its socialized medicine, do affect people's ability to take care of themselves. Couple this with the fact that persistent financial worry is a prime stressor gives us a financial view of our health concerns. To thrive we should ideally choose a career that will not subject us to ongoing bad stress or drudgery that leads to burn-out, and will also provide us with a decent income level and benefits. I know some people are laughing at the idea of "choosing" these things but that is really a matter of attitude too. If you think you can't make choices in these areas, you probably won't. In any case, we cannot afford to ignore our financial health if we want to thrive.

I called this health for our pocket book because that is the place we tend to see our financial health on a daily basis. Because financial is often the area people focus on in thinking about their "success" and because it is often the scariest area, people have very contradictory feelings and thoughts about money. I have been in debt up to my eyeballs, and I have also been well into the black. Would I go back into debt? Yes, I fully expect that to happen. Most of us, even the wealthy, cannot make a large purchase, own a house, own property or take business risks without acquiring debt. The more important question is not are you fully out of debt, but are you balancing your assets (money, income and wealth) against you liabilities (debts and expenses)? Is your debt manageable? Do you save money at the same time that you pay off debts? Do you take calculated or smart risks with money? Do most of your investments hold their value or increase their value well beyond inflation? If you are not balancing your assets against your liabilities then it would be like going out in an overloaded boat that could easily take on water.

You want to always be striving to get your assets much higher than your liabilities without compromising a good life. In other words,

I don't want people to cut back drastically and find places to pinch pennies on basics that they need to live a healthy life. Neither do I want them to rely on the dangerous temptation of credit. What people rarely do is think about how they can maximize their income, but there are many ways to do that. Learning about money and continuing to maintain that knowledge and control over your resources is a huge asset and once you have that knowledge it is not something that anyone can take away from you. They can foreclose on you, but if you have the knowledge of how to build it back you are truly rich. No doubt Scrooge, after his transformation, did not find himself giving all his profits away, but kept his business lively enough so that he could use his money to help others. No use making sure Tiny Tim is healed if he can no longer afford to pay Bob Cratchit a salary sufficient to send Tim and his other children to a good school.

What Are You Investing In?

People who are only surviving make a chronic mistake of putting their money in to small cheap "things." They tend to buy disposable things or inexpensive, but poor quality items. They rarely want to consider putting their money into important, lasting assets like education, health, or assets that increase or hold value, like good stocks, quality furniture, good hard-backed classic books, or quality timeless clothes. And by no means do I mean you necessarily want to buy new, or pay full price for material goods, no indeed. A good financial planner will warn against paying full price and full tax on new items. Go ahead, bargain-hunt and buy used goods. But still buy quality. It is also no different with investments or mortgages. It's still important to get a good price and get good advice where you retain the right amount of control and diversity in your investments. People with survival mentality are afraid of educating themselves about money and investing. They tend to make poor risks with little or no control, like lottery tickets.

Survival mentality people may have some quality things but do not have the money or inclination to care for them and unfortunately their investment may not hold its value because of that. In investing, they don't look at the fine print or don't do the all-important due diligence, because they are in a hurry to land a bargain and can't be bothered. The rule of thumb is: if it sounds too good to be true, it likely is.

When you become content that you are going to be on the planet for awhile – hopefully we all have decided we are going to be here for a few more decades –you will want to reflect that belief by investing in things that will serve you for that length of time. These do not need to be material things. As I said, health and education are two of the greatest things you can invest in. Each individual's body and mind are unique and rare; investing in them will never let you down. Even if it is time and not money you are investing, make a wise investment and recognize this as an attribute of those who thrive. Yes, you can go into debt buying too much quality furniture, books, clothes, art, or health services on credit, or have large student loans. The question is, are you balancing assets and liabilities? Are all of the things you are buying assets? Or are some liabilities? Are some depreciating and others increasing in value? Will your education propel you into better opportunities? Did it teach you invaluable things that you will use or enjoy for the rest of your life? If it didn't, I urge you: Do not give up on education.

Education

You can work without an education, but do not give up on learning, especially learning from the best. Mark Twain said, "I never let my schooling interfere with my education." This may seem like a slight against academic education, but as I see it, he is advising us to balance life experience with schooling to get the best results. Education does have a way of paying off later, even if your first experience didn't get you where you thought it would. Too many people are left with a large student loan from a degree they have never used. However, as a professional recruiter I can tell you that a BA degree on a resumé always means something. First, it means you had the persistence to finish, and second, it means that you learned the discipline and hard work that it takes to finish a degree. It means your writing skills are at a higher level than if you had not got that degree. What field it was in may be less relevant to the world than you originally thought. The great bonus about education is it is portable. Once you have it, it can never be taken from you.

Being wise in your second choice of education will serve you. You want your main education to cater to your strengths, while other bits of education may round out other useful skills. You may want to experiment with other fields of study to take you down new roads that have a pay-off or a connection, or both. If you want education to help you thrive then ideally you want it to feed your mind, your body, your soul, and your pocket book.

One of the things I recommend is to get someone else to pay for your education whenever possible. This is one of the tenets of thriving: Get Help. I don't mean student loans because you will eventually have to pay for them. Although I don't disregard the advantages of a student loan either. Student loans can represent a good debt. A debt with a future. However, what is better is to get someone else to pay for most, or all, of the tab. I mean funds from your government, from scholarships, from your parents, your company or organization -- not a loan.

Find out the parameters of your company's education policy, if it has one. If you can find something that works both for the company and your future plans, take it. There are a great number of government programs, especially for the unemployed, which are available to take advantage of. Until I took a course in Economics I did not fully realize governments' economic responsibility to get people working and make sure they are educated workers. When individuals do better, an entire country benefits. So, don't feel guilty about the government chipping in. You may have to jump through some hoops and fill out applications, but it is well worth it -- and you can even find people to help you do that. In order not to be paying out a lot for education I have also worked out bartering deals with coaches and instructors, and signed up for free mentorship programs. I use the library and all its resources extensively. I have received reductions, discounts, remissions, awards, and bursaries and extensions in Employment Insurance to cover education. I have shared text books, or found old editions to cut my education costs to the bone. Why? Because I learned the hard way how long one can be paying their student loan debts when they have not tried to reduce costs. Costs can often be cut in half or less with some research and effort. The second time, someone else paid for most of it and this was much better.

Poor Investments

If you haven't yet learned by making poor investments, you probably want to give it a small gamble. It's worth it for the lesson(s). But if you want to save a little money, and avoid some truly poor investments I will tell you what poor investments look like. One cardinal rule is: don't invest out of greed. Most poor investments are very tempting because they appear too good to be true (because they are). Invest because you are a true believer, but do lots of brass tacks research, and get feedback from others before you invest. Many poor investments have a promoter who seems crazy sure about all the money you are going to be making. Don't listen. If you can't get any more than one person's input, don't do it. Or, invest a little for the experience and fun of it. Invest because you have a plan for the future and this is not part of it. Don't invest expecting any return. Invest knowing it could be a 100% loss. And don't invest a lot.

In other words, risk what you are comfortable losing. Lots of books will tell you to go beyond your comfort zone. But for money, I say take calculated risks or not at all. I say educate yourself and your comfort zone naturally expands to what makes sense. For example many people cite the financial investment wizard Warren Buffet who does not invest in anything until he has researched and understands it thoroughly. In other words he makes a proactive effort to see if he is comfortable with something or not.

When I have a first impression that I later discover is wrong, it usually means I carried negative or positive associations into the first impression that were not based on facts. In recruiting we call a positive first impression of a candidate the "halo effect" because it is often based on superficial details. If a candidate is good looking and well groomed and likes the same hockey team as the hiring manager, or even lives in the same neighborhood, he may be hired without checking references or going through a thorough interview and analysis. The manager may feel comfortable investing in this person, but a professional recruiter might not. The same thing is true for investing money. Don't be superficial, go into detail and don't get caught up in the halo effect.

How do you educate yourself about investing? Go on-line. Read books. Watch shows. Rent DVDs. The library is one of our greatest resources. Get over the fact that you tell yourself you are not good with numbers or money. That's precisely why you need a little education. Then and only then you may want to choose a professional. They come in all styles and demeanors and choosing someone who acts like your best buddy is not always your best bet. You are the director always. That's why you get a little education and then ask a lot of questions after that of your potential professional financial advisor. They can at least organize what you already have and get you clear on some goals. But make sure they are very clear about your risk tolerances.

Your Whole Health Plan

I have now reviewed my four pillars of health for mental, physical, soulful and financial. You now have just enough information to tie your Whole Health Plan together. Do the exercise below to start you forward.

Exercise for Whole Health

Example:

Health Area	What you DO towards it	What is your motto
Mental (reading, dialogue with others, and what affects your self-esteem)	I read articles and books that expand my knowledge and help me understand my world, others and myself better. I engage people in dialogue.	"A mind open to knowledge is a mind of a powerful person."
Body (anything that affects your physical health)	I swim and dance weekly, take supplements, drink lots of water and eat healthy foods.	"My physical health comes first"
Soul (your spiritual, meditation, reflection time or artistic practice)	Dancing and listening to live music weekly.	"Art, music and dancing feed my soul"
Financial (investments for future)	I look for bargains on quality goods that can help me thrive. I look for and research good investments and good interest rates.	"Money allows me to take better care of my health and my family's health"

In the graph below, record either what you do now and want to maintain, or what you WANT to do in the near future for each of these areas.

Your Health Plan:

Health Area	What you DO towards this area of you health once a week.	What is your motto towards this area of your health.

If you are not doing something towards these health areas on a weekly basis or feel one area is weaker than others, then this is important feedback for you. Balancing your health has no compromises. It is the route to thriving and helping others thrive too. Let's recap a few of the things that may go into a Health Plan.

To recap this chapter:

Mental Health:

- ☐ Reading, playing games or regularly participating in activities that engage the mind will keep you sharp.
- ☐ Discussions and interactions with others keep you healthy.
- ☐ Limit "quick fixes."
- ☐ Balance open-mindedness with probing skepticism.
- ☐ Use professionals such as proactive coaches, naturopaths, accountants or support groups.
- ☐ Start a journal.

Physical Health:

- ☐ Do not confuse body image with body health – always focus on health and happiness together.
- ☐ Find healthy foods that also make you happy and incorporate more of them in your life.
- ☐ Find and participate in activities that make you happy – fun-outs - or that you always wanted to learn, and incorporate them into your life.

- ☐ Get enough sleep and rest.

- ☐ Get enough sexual pleasure and release – yes, you can give this to yourself.

- ☐ Add a weekly guided meditation or a breath-ritual, or use breath consciousness as needed.

- ☐ Quality in, quality out; give yourself permission to spend money on food and activities that you know your body likes (is healthy and happy).

Soul Health:

- ☐ Become aware of the sensual banquet of life that is around you daily.

- ☐ Indulge in artistic expression or appreciation.

- ☐ Drop a smooth stone in the pocket of your coat or jacket as a touchstone to help you remember the banquet.

- ☐ Find places to include joy in your daily life and share the joy with others.

- ☐ Get out of your context for a day or two, well away from your routines. Go where you can empty your soul before you fill up again.

Financial Health:

- ☐ Are you balancing your assets with your liabilities? Do you have sensible debts or is it all debt and no or little savings, investments or assets?

- ☐ Refrain from investing in poor quality things that do not retain their value or are "depreciating assets."
- ☐ Invest in things that give you a pay back, not high risk (lottery tickets)
- ☐ Invest and reinvest in your most portable and renewable resource: Education.
- ☐ Always, always do a little research in how you can get someone else to pay for your education.
- ☐ Never invest money when you are feeling too greedy. Instead invest in research and take an educated risk.
- ☐ Educate yourself about investing money by reading books, articles, renting DVDs, etc.

"Never move in the direction fear makes you move."
                    - Julaluddin Rumi - Sufi Prophet
"Motivation is what gets you started. Habit is what keeps you going."   *- John Rohn*

Chapter Seven – Fears and Habits

What's the connection between fears and habits? I can tell you that it is a very positive sign if you don't connect these two things. Habits, to most, mean something routine, familiar and boring. If it is a habit, you are not afraid of it. In many ways forging new habits will become the antidote to many fears and fears are the greatest things that hold us back. The problem is, the specter of fear arises every time we try something new. For each kind of fear the negative-speak and rationalizations will be different, but there are ways to get over those first hurdles. You can break down the thing you fear into smaller habits that you can forge, become comfortable with, and will move you over even your biggest fears, but first let's talk about fear.

Let's Talk About Fear

In order to deal with anything, like elephants, you have to name it and then focus on it. Although I was already aware that I had fears, I did not really understand what fear was, until a fortunate coincidence occurred.

At the night school where I had been teaching both creative and business writing, the programmer asked me if I would teach a *Fear of Writing* course which had been previously taught by another popular teacher who was leaving. I jumped at the chance, thinking this was something I knew something about. As I have said before, teaching something is the best way to learn it. First, I had to do my research into the subject, second, I had to analyze more deeply my own experiences of it, and third I had to listen closely to others' experiences, including the first students who came in the door looking to face a fear of writing. In teaching the course, not only did I change the course name to *Writing with Cold Feet*, I learned more and more about fear of writing as well as fear in general. I learned that while most people who came to this course did have fears of grammar and of being judged, which were issues I was already prepared to tackle in my course, most of what I heard people describe was not fear, but blatant procrastination. So I did more research, listened more, and confronted my own procrastination.

This work culminated in my producing another course, *Putting Off Procrastination.* There are many theories and treatments such as cognitive behaviour therapy extolled by experts in "task avoidance" but I came to like the "procrastination styles" work that Dr. Linda Sapadin put forward. She went into what went behind the procrastination, and the fact that self-awareness is always the precursor to any change. But I was also impressed with the Zen teachings of Cheri Huber, which were new to me also. She connected fears and procrastination to both your programming and, more importantly, to your self-esteem.

Fear and Programming

Quite often fears and even procrastination are programmed responses. By that I mean you mimic your parents or older siblings, or listen to their cautions that were meant to be protective in nature. There is often at least one parent who was very concerned with security and did not venture to try things. Although you may feel you do not you take after that parent, and you are your own person and very different, there may be warnings still stuck in your head that bring up feelings of trepidation whenever you are in certain situations. My mother, who was pretty much always a secure, stay-at-home housewife and did not know anything of today's job markets would freak out whenever she found out I was between jobs. She would say to me, "You'd better find something or you're going to be out on the street!" Yes, her fears were that extreme. I simply stopped telling her any more if I was between jobs. When I became entrepreneurial, I would talk about clients as if they were my employers, which they were, and she never caught on that I was taking new risks that she would never dare to take. I did this to protect myself, as much as protect her. I did not want her pushing an age-old fear button she had planted in me.

Part of tackling fears is being aware of your familial programming, but programming also comes from schools. For my term project in Education in university I made a documentary video, returning to my old elementary school (grades one through seven), with permission to interview and photograph the children on their lunch break. The project was to study what activities and games kids did during their lunch breaks and recesses. Were little boys differed from little girls? Did activities change as they approached high school?

In grades one and two I found that the girls and boys played together freely and unselfconsciously, playing such games as freeze tag and games that they had creatively made up themselves around a piece of playground equipment. In these games, the rules were created and agreed upon by all the children. They were self-governing and dealt with their own conflicts independent of an adult authority. As they went up the grades, the boys started to play adult-governed sports like hockey and soccer with other boys only. Winning and losing against an opposing side became more important, particularly for the boys. The girls continued to play creative games, such as skip-rope, with its old oral tradition of skip-rope songs.

In the final grade before they left elementary school the girls abruptly stopped skip-rope and other creative games. They told me that they had scouted out what girls do in high school and they now began to be spectators for the boys. A few also became interested in playing sports. What is my point about this programming? For this chapter, my point is that our programming tells us what we are "supposed to do" but, unfortunately it can also set up blocks that don't help us cope with the ebb and flow of life later on.

Games in which there are clear winners and losers sets up little boys to make winning the ultimate, important goal in life. This is mirrored in professional sports. For many this is inspirational, but for many others, it is a form of pressure which gives them a profound "fear of losing." I find this in young men, whether they were good at sports, or not sports-oriented at all. Girls, on the other hand, were more likely to be slow to take risks and often went through an early identity crisis, but felt less pressure about winning and losing. Keep in mind that this was research I did over fifteen years ago, and now girls are being socialized more like the boys than ever before, although the same early patterns do exist.

In order for you to move into thriving easily, be aware that winning is not a god and losing is not a great shame. While competition is not an evil concept, I have heard successful entrepreneurs say that persistence is more important, along with the ability to adapt, change, learn and bounce back from misfortunes and failures, than the ability to win or to be super competitive. A successful entrepreneur friend of mine put it succinctly when he said, "You have to be able to make adversity your friend." Your ability to self-govern, without clear direction or rules, which was once an early skill in the playground, becomes a valuable tool that you can now return to. Your ability to balance having fun while creating and accomplishing is also an important ability to take away from earlier days at the playground and one that helps you move away from fears of failure.

Fear and Self-Esteem

Higher self-esteem does not eliminate fears, however higher self-esteem enables a person to go forward despite fears. The famous saying by Franklin D. Roosevelt "the only thing we have to fear is fear itself," suggests the power of the internal enemy, fear. Fear can be motivated by some immediate threat, but much more often it is motivated by our own thoughts. Self-esteem is like the penicillin for fear. Or maybe a better analogy is that strong self-esteem is the healthy immune system against an infection of fear. Fear starts as a minor infection but with a healthy self-esteem can be quashed and put in its appropriate place before it grows to a very nasty and sometimes crippling infection. It's the best tool we have for a healthy, happy, thriving life. Building self-esteem also means abandoning previous negative programming and replacing it with positive and for this you have to start with awareness. Awareness of any kind can give you the impetus to try a different route. Reprogramming and building both self-esteem and better habits, are a continuous, successive process. But I have learned that as you go through the process, some systematic steps can help you put fear in reverse gear.

Put Fear in Reverse Gear

To face your fears right away, you may need to break them down into steps. For true fears it is always the first step towards going forward that is the hardest to make. It usually involves some sort of "showing up" as Woody Allen said. That can mean showing up to a meeting, an interview, a class, picking up the phone, opening a book, approaching a person, or turning on a computer and logging on. Showing up means taking the first step. To get there psychologically I developed an acronym to remember my method for putting fear in reverse gear, which is RAEF, that's fear spelled backwards.

1. Reassurance
2. Awareness & 3. Evaluation
4. Forward

Reassurance

When we were little it was okay if we fell down as we learned. That was normal. But, for some reason we don't like this as adults. Because we no longer have parents or adults right at the ready to reassure us that this thing that is new to us, this fear, will turn out okay, we need to reassure ourselves. But, if we are to move on to thriving, we know that even when events do not turn out okay -- even when we fall down a lot -- we can learn valuable lessons. Learning is the achievement meant for everything. Again, the thriving success attitude is: Learning Is the Achievement Meant for Everything.

But because we still feel the pain of learning and growing, and the anxiety of the unfamiliar, we first need to give ourselves reassurance that facing something new will be worthwhile. I remember musing with my friend Irwin Barker, a comic and television comedy writer, about this subject. We were trying to imagine a comedic look at what it must have been like for the first caveman who walked upright. How difficult was it for him to talk the other cavemen into trying it? "Come on, you gotta try it, it's really great." But every time they would try it, they would fall down and give up. So, the one cave man who had mastered it had to really pester his friends or try to trick them into standing up. Irwin thought it might make a funny sketch, but I was interested in the fact that all human accomplishments, small and great, start the way we imagined that scene. People are suspicious and ready to give up on something new and unfamiliar. As far as taking first steps upright, we all reproduce that historic accomplishment in our first year of life. You've gotten this far, as has the whole human race, so chances are you can reassure yourself that whatever fear you face, it has been faced already, and overcome by many. It too can become as simple the habit of walking upright.

At 38, I decided I wanted to learn how to rollerblade because it looked like such fun and I live near Stanley Park, a large city park with a 5.5-mile paved seawall around the perimeter. It is one of the most beautiful scenic walks in Vancouver and in fact in the world. Now I have mastered the basics of rollerblading and I skate the seawall frequently in under an hour, for the sheer joy of it. I like to rollerblade quite fast and I rarely think of falling. But when I try to talk to people who don't or won't rollerblade but would like to, they always voice the same fear: fear of falling. Lord knows, when I began I was afraid of falling and being embarrassed. The strange thing is, I know that these same people who have the fear – just like I did – are far too conservative and prudent to do anything reckless that could cause a truly nasty fall. These people will practice in a flat easy area. They won't try to go down hills until they have mastered balance. These people will get lessons, and the first thing they teach you in lessons is how to fall so you won't hurt yourself (it makes me wonder if that first upright caveman had to give lessons). My point is that the fear is worse than the event, and you can always work out solutions to thwart the fear step by step. But first you have to reassure yourself that it's never going to be that bad. If you need help from others to help reassure and encourage you, then seek out the people who will. Listen to encouraging words from everyone. One of my friends says she has to say to herself before facing any fear, "It's not going to kill me." When facing a fear, say whatever it takes to reassure yourself. You are the adult here, and you are also the toddler. When you decide to face a fear say to yourself the most encouraging and reassuring words you can think of. Banish as much negativity as possible. For example, rather than saying "I will not fall." I started to say to myself, "I have good balance."

Awareness and Evaluation

I put Awareness and Evaluation together because they are very connected parts of the process. Awareness comes first because you will want to be aware of what you are actually afraid of. In rollerblading, one may fear falling, but for many the embarrassment of falling in front of others is far worse than the fear of falling itself. Knowing what your actual fear is, gives you the power to tackle it. Someone I know dealt with this fear by having private, one-to-one lessons, out of the view of others. Another very outgoing friend of mine told me that she was already aware she had a fear of selling that she wanted to face. Though she did not need the money she decided to take a part-time sales job where the company agreed to train her. In the process, she figured out that her real fear wasn't simply the fear of selling, nor the fear of being rejected that many have about sales. Her real fear was that she could not handle people's objections to the sale. In the successive process of facing a fear, she had to evaluate her fear to get down to the nitty-gritty. When you can evaluate, you can put a successful strategy on your fear. She was able to focus and practice in the area of handling objections. In my first Fear of Writing classes, when we discovered that the students' fears were mostly procrastination rather than an immediate present fear (it's hard to fall down at your word processor), it gave us a strategy to focus on some habit-forming techniques that worked for procrastination.

In your awareness and evaluation, you will also want to focus on the benefits that facing this fear will bring to you. Facing each fear will improve your life, and you must repeat the benefits so that you can clearly understand them. The benefits won't destroy the fear, but must outweigh the fear. Many find it beneficial to make a pros-and-cons list in their evaluation. At times I have faced fears simply because I was told to do so, or I was under peer pressure. I don't recommend this as ideal. Although sometimes it worked out, other times it had disastrous results. If you want to do something, but are feeling trepidation about it, or are under pressure to do it, take some time to think of how it is going to benefit you personally, not anyone else's agenda. For me, if it is a physical challenge, I have to watch and observe people doing whatever it is several times before I am ready. This reassures me and also gives me time to remind myself of the benefits. The thriving person must see the clear gain and keep reminding themselves of that gain.

Forward

Awareness and evaluation alone won't destroy the fear, so the only way to destroy the fear is to act. You must put into action the thing you are afraid of. For most fears, you not only have to do it, you have to keep doing it, until you have developed a habit. Sometimes there will always be fear even when you have done things repeatedly. I know veteran performers who still experience stage fright, but for most, stage fright turns into exhilaration, or at worst a controlled, nervous anticipation.

My technique for going forward each time you experience fear is to start by reassuring yourself. Keep an awareness of your actual fear and that it is conquerable, and keep reminding yourself in your evaluation of its clear benefits. I use this self-talk: "I will be better for going forward." I use self-talk that tells me that this fear isn't proven, it is just a fear. When I am rollerblading where there are a lot of obstacles, rough surfaces or debris, again, I reassure myself that "I have great balance." I let myself know that if I stumble, I can regain my balance. Frankly, I don't know if I have great balance, but rollerblading for years has probably improved my balance.

Exercise

Going Forward

If you are in the U.S. Airborne today, or were in one of the famous battalions that accomplished amazing feats in the Second World War, they still yell "Geronimo!" as they jump out of their planes with their parachutes. This was started by a young paratrooper to show fearlessness in the face of jumping. He and others in his platoon had just seen the Hollywood movie about Geronimo, a film that honors the great Apache Chief. Geronimo was an amazing warrior who was able to win battles against American soldiers even when his weapons were more primitive, and he was outnumbered ten to one or more. Even if you don't like war stories this is a very impressive accomplishment. It is interesting to me that the Airborne paratrooper chose to adopt the courage and the determination implied in the name of a famous warrior chief as his way to send himself off before the very nerve-racking prospect of jumping out of a plane and into a dangerous mission. Through this story I realized that all of us can have a Geronimo yell (or saying) that we give before we move forward that gives us our last-ditch courage and sends us off. Remember my friend who says, "It's not going to kill me," before doing the thing that she fears. A Geronimo yell means there is no going back, only forward, and you do it every time you feel the fear and jump anyway.

I have started a list of the last thing you might say before you jump, some are clichés, some from movies, some from people I know and others are my own. You can borrow one of these or develop your own.

- "It's not going to kill me,"
- "Geronimo!"
- "I'm game."
- "Damn the torpedoes and full speed ahead."
- "Forward."
- "There's no looking back."
- "We're on a mission from God"
- "Carpe diem." or "Seize the day"
- "Time to chew bubblegum and kick ass."
- "You've come a long way baby."

- ☐   "Next!"
- ☐   "Here goes nothing."
- ☐   "Let's get busy."
- ☐   "Away we go."
- ☐   "Just watch me."
- ☐   "Hi-Yo Silver..away!"
- ☐   "What the hell."
- ☐   "Let's make some cookies."
- ☐   "Go baby, go."
- ☐   One for You: _____
- ☐   One for You: _____
- ☐   One for You: _____

Let's Talk About Making New Habits

"Good habits, once established are just as hard to break as are bad habits" – Robert Porter

As I said earlier if you make things into habits you will lose both fears and procrastinations. It's a great idea to start with small things and prove that you can make new habits. And, you can make a habit of creating good habits. Creating a daily routine or habit of some kind takes effort, but only at the beginning. You need to be able to focus on it. Most people try to make changes without focusing on the small habits that guide them into change. This is a basic 5-step formula I call APT TO as in you are "apt to" do it.

1. **Awareness.** That word again. Again ask your self: Why do I want to do this? How will it make my life better? Avoid answering, "because I *should* do it", or "because I will be punished if I don't." Instead, identify a clear benefit or benefits to you and state them clearly, simply and positively. You don't have to go into every possible reason, just the main ones.

2. **Preparation.** What are the things you need to do to prepare to focus on this task? This can number many or few but you will want to make a list. When you haven't started your habit yet, and you are just tiptoeing around it and cataloguing, *lists are your best friends.* In some ways preparation is a positive form of procrastinating. Don't think about doing it yet, just think about the list and only the list, and keep repeating, "This is doable. I'll prepare for it." I frequently make an agreement with myself to make these lists on the commercial breaks of a favorite TV show.

Whatever time-pocket that you can find, use it get the list or other preparation done.

3. **Timeline Commitment.** As a default I always commit to doing the things I want to make into daily habits for a minimum of three weeks, like making the bed, so it will become a habit. If it is a one-time achievement the timeline end date may obviously vary. For things that are not daily accomplishments, like doing your taxes, there are three other rules for timeline success.

    a. Start on some aspect of the chore on the day you make your commitment, or, at the latest, the very next day. Whether it's making a list or some other aspect (it does not have to be in order) do something towards it to start. Like Scrooge on Christmas Day after seeing the spirits, strike while the iron is hot to make the changes real.

    b. Make the final end date realistic. Not too far ahead, which does not help procrastinators, and not too soon that it is truly unrealistic.

    c. Don't beat yourself up if you need to extend the end date – notice I like to call them end dates rather than deadlines. Nobody dies, you just get back on track. Think of timelines as lifelines, not deadlines

When I told my partner the specific end date that I had for finishing the first draft of this book, he asked if that was my deadline or the editors. I said, "It's always my date. I'm the only one who cares." To a certain extent that is true, you are the only one that these timelines really matter to. They are going to make a difference to your life. It may affect others, others may demand things of you, but if the life that it's going to make better is yours, you are going to want to care about the timelines.

4. **Training - Get Your Muscles and Mind Auto-Remembering.** If this is a repeating daily habit that you are trying to create, and even if it is temporary project, it will involve some kind of repetition. Our mind and muscles love repetition and will use any rituals of repetition to feel comforted, reassured and move forward. This is called training. Training may not rid people of fears but it will make them do it despite the fear and do it better. Many of our repetitions can also be transposed onto anything similar like my dinner party to public event planning. First, find or create the repetition or ritual preparation parts. Then, find the "spring board" thing you need to start doing first. This can be as simple as making a list, booting up the computer, taking out the tools you will be using, cleaning up, calling a

meeting, or doing the first preparation items. These actions often are similar and repetitious for any project and signal the start of action. Being aware of these two things, how you start, what you will have to repeat, is how you create your training program. Write down what gets you started, and what keeps you on track. This is process. The rest will flow naturally towards product. Theater troupes often use ensemble-building exercises to start rehearsals and the whole process of repetition and rehearsals keeps everyone on track. Many directors remind a troupe that opening night is only another dress rehearsal, to reassure them that they are ready, and remind them that they have done their training, and continue to do their habit of rehearsal. This is a way to ease any tension – reassurance for putting fear in reverse gear!

5. **Over-praise - Recognize the Inherent Reward with Self Talk.** Be proud of yourself as you are accomplishing anything towards your goal. Tell yourself how clever you are to do this. Repeat the benefits of how this habit will make your life happier and healthier. Tell yourself you are thriving when you do this new habit. Tell yourself you are never going back to leaving it undone. You cannot overdo praise of yourself. Avoid whining and complaining, as in "Why do I have to do this….I hate doing this." Remember,

your unconscious believes everything it hears. If you want your mind to remember that this process was hard going, go ahead and complain to yourself, and I guarantee you will find it hard to repeat this task, or any new task every time you try one. The less you tell yourself you dislike it, and the more you over-praise yourself, the easier it will become every time.

The tables below demonstrate two different kinds of new habits we want to form using the APT TO method. The first one is a simple habit of never losing your keys. The second is a larger project we love to procrastinate on: doing your taxes.

APT TO Project: Never Lose Keys				
Awareness	Preparation	Timeline Commitment	Training	Over-praise
Why do you want to do this?	Where do the keys go?	How long am I going to commit to creating this habit?	What training do I have to do?	How am I going to praise myself?

I recognize that being able to quickly locate my keys saves me time.	Prepare a place to habitually leave keys, like a hook or a dish.	For three weeks, I commit to daily putting my keys in only these two places. END DATE: August 15	Every time I touch my keys, when I leave or enter, I have to put them in the right place.	Every time I find or put my keys in the correct place, I will be proud and...
Quickly locating my keys reduces my stress.	When away from home, keys go in the same pocket /place	I give myself license to extend the deadline – whoops, lifeline	If I goof, I take the time to put it where it belongs.	I am clever to save time. It makes me happy. I am thriving

Think APT TO is silly and obvious? Maybe, but silly and obvious works better when you break it down and have an awareness. The trick is to start with something small and doable that you realize has importance. Then move on to other habits. The same formula will work for many things that cause you procrastination and anxiety. Let's try something harder and bigger, but that is not a daily task. Let's APT TO doing your taxes.

APT TO Project: Do taxes				
Aware-ness	Preparation	Timeline Commitment	Training	Over-praise
Why do you want to do this?	**What do I need to do?**	**What is my timeline commitment?**	**What training do I have to do?**	**How am I going to praise myself?**
I get a refund promptly to put towards a vacation	Look at the tax website to discover the best way to make a fast return.	By mid-January I will look at government website	Review last year's taxes. Familiar with website or software.	This habit makes me happier, healthier and wealthier.
I want control over my finances	Buy tax software. Get friend or pro to help.	By end of January complete preparation.	I am going to boot up software and use the help.	I am going to boast to others that I've done my taxes.
I am able to do this.	Find all my receipts.	Mid February gather all my receipts.	Train to put my receipts in a labelled file as they come in.	I am so clever to have created new files and have a system
I am the best person to do this.	Start filling in the easy things on the forms	Mid Feb (start on form)	Do 10 minutes a day on software	I love myself every step I take

Aware-ness	Preparation	Timeline Commitment	Training	Over-praise
I want to never be afraid of it!	Get someone to check it over for me or use software / online tools	Submit taxes by March 1	Practice asking for help or using on-line help as needed.	I am proud of myself for getting my taxes done so soon.
I want to get the process so efficient it feels like no big deal	Create a paper and e-file for this year and next year.	Clean up files by March 5	Help someone else with theirs to help reinforce your learning	I am so smart to have the refund back!

APT TO: Awareness, preparation, timelines, training, and over-praising may not be something you will want to do every time you want to get something done, but it is a great place to start if you find you have a lot of resistance to doing what has been hanging over you. When working in the area of procrastination, studies have shown that people's anxiety increases the more they stall on a project or problem. But, the sooner they act – even in small ways - the sooner the weight comes off their shoulders. You will find that procrastination will generally melt away the more positively you feel about yourself and talk about yourself. You will also find that the more you work on small daily habits the easier it may be to tackle larger fears.

To recap:

- ☐ Both self-esteem building and positive self-talk will help dissolve fears and reinforce positive habits.
- ☐ Put Fear In Reverse Gear use: RAEF: Reassurance, Awareness Evaluation and Forward.
- ☐ Use a Geronimo saying to help you move forward.
- ☐ To understand fears, be aware of your programming and consider that you may want to overcome it.
- ☐ What are you really afraid of? Evaluate. Get to the nitty-gritty, so you can build a precise strategy to deal with it.
- ☐ Habits are the antidotes to fear.
- ☐ Remind yourself of the gain. What are you gaining by facing this fear or by creating this habit?
- ☐ Use APT TO to create a positive habit. Awareness, Preparation, Timeline, Training and Over-praise.
- ☐ It usually takes three weeks every day to get your mind and muscles on autopilot to create a positive daily habit.
- ☐ Lists are your best friends. Make them during the commercial b of your favorite TV shows.
- ☐ You are the only one to care about the timelines.
- ☐ Don't beat yourself up if you get off track, just get back on.

Chapter Eight - Career <u>vs.</u> Relationship?

My father likes to say, there are two kinds of people, those who divide people into two kinds, and those who don't. Such is the humor of my father. But, I guess I fall into the former kind of people because I have noticed that by and large there are often two groups of people, one group of people who uses relationships to avoid thriving in their careers, and another group who uses their career/work obligations to avoid thriving in their relationships.

When I say this, I don't mean that they are necessarily doing it consciously. Some are and some are not, but they all claim not to be getting what they really want. There are both men and women out there who say they will not have time for a relationship until their careers are where they want them to be. Equally, there are men and women out there who expend a great deal of energy trying to find an "ideal" or "perfect" mate, or trying to fix a hopeless relationship, while ignoring their career. I find it interesting that for many people this has unintentionally become a society of Career versus Relationship. Some people swear that they are okay with their career, it's just the love relationship they can't get right, others say they have the relationship, but they hate their career. Let's face it, many of us are having trouble with both. All of these people are usually blinding themselves to the truth.

I myself spent far too much time trying to fix hopeless relationships, usually with men whose careers or jobs came first, and who were traveling for great chunks of the year. As a consequence, neither my career nor my relationships flourished. This was not just my problem. It was also dovetailing perfectly with the problem of the person who I was trying to have a relationship with. People have a strong tendency to link up with other people who are avoiding the opposite thing. Why? Again, it goes back to our fears. We don't have to truly practice the thing that scares us (while it also attracts us), so it gives us a sense of control, even when we are out of control and cheating ourselves of doing better than we could. It also goes back to victim mentality and not growing up. It may take two to dance the crazy non-functioning relationship tango, however, it only takes one to grow up and make it work for the one.

Women, especially if they were born in the fifties, sixties or seventies, often link relationships with security. Men can do this too, at any age, but security may mean something different to them. Security is linked to whatever we experienced as secure in childhood as well as the messages that society gives us. For many women, security meant or means being taken care of financially. For many men, the same thing is true about feeling secure in a relationship; he may have a sense of being taken care of emotionally and physically. Some people want both but usually they want to find someone else to take care of the scary things, or the things someone (their parents) always did for them. Or the contrary, they are afraid that they will be put in a situation where they are possibly controlled by someone parent-like. The problem with either mentality, whether you have it to a small degree or a large degree, is that it puts adults back into a childhood state.

Women and men both link career to a masculine power base. It is a place of control, but mostly it is a place of status. It is a place where you can find out the rules and move up the status ladder. This is true to a greater or lesser degree in any field,. For some individuals this is highly attractive, especially the control aspect. For the same individuals, intimacy or one-to-one close relationships are disturbing because they represent a loss of control, something they fear may take them back to a childhood state, in a negative sense. This is a state where they fear they are being controlled by a parent-like individual. You can see how someone who wants to be financially supported is attracted to the career-minded person, yet it is also appealing to the person who is afraid of intimacy, because they can look after that individual and feel like they *are* the parent rather than being parented. Their fears dovetail perfectly, at first. Unfortunately, this relationship doesn't go far in rewarding either individual. One becomes too clingy in the relationship and the other becomes too distant and goes back into the safer haven of workaholic habits. They cannot grow or thrive if they do not look at what each is avoiding.

For Those Avoiding Career

Are you a person who wants badly to be in a relationship and spends a lot of your time thinking about this? Do you want to be in a relationship because of an emotional need for love? If in a relationship, are you spending more time and effort on your relationship than on your career? Are you avoiding the scariness of financial security and thriving in the outside world? If so, is it time to take your head out of the sand and start taking care of business and facing those fears? Here are some questions for you to answer:

☐ Have you ever done a budget?

☐ Do you know where almost every dollar goes, every month, and have you ever documented this to confirm it?

☐ Do you know how much you want to be making, after taxes, each month or each year in order to feel like you are thriving?

☐ Are you out of debt?

☐ Are you saving or investing?

☐ Have you found a career versus a job? Or planned to get education for a career?

☐ Have you focused on a career that you are reasonably sure you will enjoy, and will meet all of your financial needs and wants (thriving)?

☐ Have you ever dropped out of a promising career because when it got rocky you gave up and moved on to something less threatening? Would you consider going back if you could get over the challenges or fears?

It is my experience and the experience of others I have met that relationship-needy people don't tend to be sensible money people. They really would rather delegate earning the money to other people and just spend the money, too often all of it. This has nothing to do with education level or intelligence. Money is very tied up with emotions, and people frequently do not want to have an appropriate understanding of it. The trouble is, you should never be prepared to totally delegate your finances to others. The more you can learn the stronger you will be. The more you learn about where you are spending money and how you choose to save it, the more in-control you will be. You will be less needy. Therefore, if you are single, the more desirable you will be and if you are not single, the less dependent on your relationship you will be. This makes for a stronger relationship that is more likely to last. You will be able to focus on the fun of doing the things you love to do together.

In order to accomplish this you need to read some easy books on budgeting, saving, getting out of debt, and financing, as already outlined in the Financial Health chapter. You would also do well to get some good career counseling. Interview some people in different careers to see what will work for you and what is the best way to get your foot in the door. These people may tell you the downsides too, so make sure you talk to more than one person and see if there is agreement on what the compensation is like and what the downsides are. You also want to talk to someone who loves their career and see if the strengths that have helped them succeed are attributes you can bring to the table as well. In other words, find out what you have and don't have and what you will need. As well, find out if it is a good time to get into that career, and if it is likely to stay that way for a few years. Find out how long it takes to get a career off the ground.

When I got into Human Resources it was a hot market. I was able to parlay my first contract position into a permanent position in a much larger company fairly rapidly, with only a minimum amount of schooling. Unfortunately this was followed by a huge slump in the economy with a lot of downsizing in which many HR people, including me, were the first to be let go . This, however, was a perfect opportunity to return to school and get my fully certified HR schooling paid for by the government, which has a vested interest in getting people back to work. While I was finishing school I picked up two independent clients, and by the time I had completed school, the economy was starting to rebound.

The moral to this story is to choose a career while there are good opportunities. Just get in there. If you are good at it and you love it, you will be able to get by in it through thick and thin. If you are paying attention to your finances and reading the right books, you will learn to prepare for any dips in the marketplace to get you through the thin times. Remember, the government has a vested interest in keeping you employed, so use their resources when you can, as long as you are not slacking and simply using the government to take care of you. That can be another way of reverting to childhood.

For Those Avoiding Relationships for Career
(even if they don't think they are)

The problem with trying to talk to the people who are avoiding relationship for career is that they often don't think they are. They do have relationships. Relationships for them just don't really get off the ground. And they don't necessarily have a stellar career either but they do spend a lot of time at work or with another passion. The symptoms are varied for these individuals so check how many questions below fit to see if you may be one of them.

- ☐ You are looking for a "soul-mate"
- ☐ You are a bit of a workaholic, (and/or may have a driving passion that takes most of your time).
- ☐ You travel a lot for your work.
- ☐ You are pretty fussy about what she/he looks like – you have favorite physical types.
- ☐ You have rejected people before because of little things they do (think *Seinfeld* characters, there is "always something").

- You have more than once felt claustrophobic in a relationship.

- You really like your freedom and you like excitement – you don't want to be bored.

- You have a lousy relationship track record and perhaps an unhappy marriage that lasted a few years or less and ended badly, and you are not on great terms with your ex.

- You fear giving up or giving in to another – you don't want to lose control.

- You don't want someone to be too dependent on you.

- In the past, you have chosen people too young for you, too old for you, or with different values, religious beliefs or views on children that eventually broke you two apart, but you knew of these differences from the start.

- You have been described as passive-aggressive.

If you think that any one of the above statements describes you, you may want to consider what you are doing, and realize that in order to have a real relationship you may need to change. Pick up some information on commitment conflicts or commitment-phobia in relationships. Yes, you may have made commitments before but something is blocking you from choosing a person you can really settle with. You may have to adjust your work habits that you have never made before. You may have to find a person better suited to your own background or stage in life. You are going to want to do some work on your own fears of intimacy and bonding if you really want a relationship as well as a career. You may also want to start believing that you can realistically have both if you change your workaholic ways. Stop working harder on the career and start working smarter. Often the results improve both arenas.

What to Do Now?

In a sense, a career-versus-relationship separation can have a positive side. That is, if no one is in your life now, it allows you the time, reflection and focus to prepare for letting either a career or a relationship happen, whichever one is eluding you. People run to the things that they can easily control or are comfortable for them. It is a hard habit to break. Why should they throw any extra, valuable time away when they know what they want and can rationalize that they simply haven't found it yet. Yet, they have already tried it that way and it hasn't been working. So, here are some good reasons for change that people of either orientation can understand.

1. If you have a career focus and are already succeeding there, then nurturing yourself to become a great, stable-relationship person gives you the power to take greater

risks in all aspects of your life, including your career. Possibilities open up. Your network opens up. You become stronger knowing there is always someone you trust in your corner making your life better. Why not put more power and more happiness in your court?

2. If you have a relationship focus, then working to find a vocation or business that gives you more energy and financial health will give you more stability and control than just a relationship can. Your financial independence will make you very attractive to many and give you the greater security that choice brings. Why not put more power and more happiness in your court?

If you think you are in one of these complementary relationships where one of you is avoiding career and the other is avoiding relationship, then the bad news is that it is sometimes difficult to work on these issues while in this relationship, but the good news is that it is not impossible and may even work out better in the end. You just have to remember one critical rule: work on your own stuff. You are changing yourself, not the other person. Remember, when you change, others change in response. Sometimes this will be a favorable change in your relationship and sometimes it won't. It may initiate a rebirth of the relationship, or a definitive end to it. But also if that happens, it means that the end was needed. When your self-esteem is higher, it forces others to examine their own. It can lead them by example, or it can confuse and frighten them as they confront a distasteful low self-esteem in themselves. But, you cannot change them; you can only change yourself.

Going Through Adversity with Someone

One of the challenges of both careers and relationships is they are both things you have to do with others. They will not always go smoothly, and there should be some conflicts that result in better understanding or better ways of operating. But in order to thrive there has to be more gain than loss; you have to have a continual increase (however gradual) in good working energy. In both work relationships and personal relationships there has to be a good base of a common belief, respect, compatibility, and commitment, or it won't last. Or, it may last, but it will never thrive. That said, you will go through challenges, obstacles, conflicts and adversity together that may be tough, but are healthy and positive. With the right attitude, difficult times build a bond and greater trust. So don't give up on your relationships or your career because of the struggles alone; you may be on the verge of growing a little deeper. Finding an ideal relationship or career isn't a question of simply finding the right person, company or field, it is a question of willingness to do something better than you ever have before.

A turning-point incident in one of my important relationships taught me a great deal. One day, I got upset at one of my best friends, whom I had known for ten years. I accused her of not trusting me, or sharing with me enough, even though I had stuck by her through thick and thin for a decade. She was very upset and ran out of the room. The next day we talked and she told me that although she didn't seem to trust me or share enough with me, out of everyone in her life I was the one person she trusted the most and shared the most with. A light went on for me and I realized that my expectations for her had been unrealistic, and I didn't need to be upset. I had thought that I wasn't valued or trusted as a friend, but, in fact, I was highly valued and trusted, but I didn't understand that she was not used to being asked to trust and share so much. Shortly after this, both of us went through a very trying experience when a mutual friend of ours went through a near fatal crisis that lasted several weeks and we really needed each other for support. Because of this experience we gained a better understanding of our different points of view, and suddenly we had the greater sharing and trust I had been wanting.

There was also an appreciation on my part that the greater trust and sharing wasn't something that I was entitled to, but that it was a gift, a great gift. This conflict worked to deepen our relationship in a way that I had never realized it could. I assumed that relationships don't change after ten years and it never occurred to me they could get better, closer and deeper. I thought the only alternative at that stage of a relationship was that it got a bit boring and stale, and if anything you might grow away from each other. Instead I learned that adversity could be a blessing, and open communication a great tool. Understanding and accepting another person is a key to depth and thriving in a relationship. It was a lesson that would later bring greater understanding to my romantic relationship and all my relationships.

It was interesting for me to learn from Jim Collins' book *Good to Great* what makes a company able to go from good to great. The book researched the attributes of companies which made changes for the better, became "great" companies, and maintained that greatness for over 15 years. One of the numerous attributes of the quality of such companies was getting the right people together. However, it didn't have to mean that these people got along wonderfully. One of the attributes were they did have conflict. The right people were committed and passionate and had different opinions that they were prepared to go to bat for. In the formative years of those changes, there is a phase people in HR call storming. The phases are forming, storming, norming and performing. There needs to be storming and conflict to root out the best solutions and figure out who is best suited to do what. If you want people who agree with you, you are not creating a dynamic and creative enough environment to go from good to great. On the other side, sometimes many companies get stuck in storming and never get to norming let alone performing. Why this happens has many answers unique to each company, but the point is, storming itself is normal and healthy as long as you are going through it.

What Old Mythologies To Let Go Of

Another reason people are not going forward in their careers or their relationships is that they need to let go of the mythologies they have been keeping alive for years. When I say mythologies I mean the memories of past events that we have spun into stories and keep repeating to ourselves and others. We tell ourselves that this is the truth. I want to expose you to something radical here. Some of the stories and truths you have been telling yourself are not truths, and neither are they lies What they are is beliefs you have chosen. Again, you have the power of choice. Let me give you examples of how we do this in large and small ways, and hold ourselves back in our career and relationship choices.

I know a woman in her fifties who would dearly love a life partner in her senior years. Over the past twenty years she has averaged two different relationships or involvements per year. When talking to her she tells me the story of her first marriage that ended after ten years with the tragic death of her partner. She was young when they first met and she says that she knew the first moment that she saw him. She just knew this was the one. There was absolutely no doubt in her mind. Naturally, it takes time to get over that loss, but she was sure she had completely achieved that. After all, she had had several other relationships since. When I probed further about her first marriage and relationship I discovered that there had been drug abuse that had made their relationship hell for most of the marriage and was the reason that they had only one child. She was so afraid that either of them might hurt a child when high, she refused to have more. They were finally getting treatment and straightening out their chaotic life when tragically her husband died. The death was completely unexpected and not drug related. It was a credit to her that she continued to be clean and sober after the trauma and went on to successfully raise their daughter alone.

The story starts now with her failed attempts to forge new relationships. Despite the mess that she had been in with her first husband, she refuses to see it as anything other than idyllic bond of soul mates. Things had gotten better in their relationship at the end, but most long-term relationships, especially forged when you are young are bound to go through adversity, albeit some more than others. But what she described still did not sound that special to me. Also, initial relationships will be seen through the childlike eyes of innocence and want to be seen as special, eternal and fateful. Couple this with society's own mythologies of the "one and only" and it is easy to understand one of the major reasons she is not maintaining her relationships. It is important for her to have loving memories of her first husband and the father of her child, but the mythology that she spins also makes it so exclusive that no one who comes along after him can measure up. The fact that the life they led for most of their marriage was by all evidence far from ideal makes me wonder why she wants so desperately to hang on to this mythology. In fact, if she truly "knew" at first sight all the things that would happen in that marriage, very likely she might have headed for the hills. There can be many reasons why she persists in this story, especially when surrounded by a history of drug abuse, but the refusal to let go of the mythology is still an essential block to moving forward on the relationship front.

Small mythologies you tell yourself also keep you from opening the door to more possibilities in your careers. "I hate computers and technology" is one I have heard people say. Now this is very different from saying "I know I don't want to spend most of my day in front of a computer." One limits your career choices, and the other focuses your career choices. Very few jobs do not involve technology and computers these days. Very few people will not be using technology in their personal lives to a great degree as well.

I hear people say "I'm not a detail person," "I don't like getting my hands dirty," or "I am terrible with numbers." Are these people simply recognizing and accepting their true nature, or are they limiting themselves? Sometimes it is a bit of both. It is important, when you catch yourself saying blanket statements about yourself, to analyze whether it is the truth, or a mythology that you have chosen. For example, most people may not be good with details, but in order to do their jobs well they have to learn to organize and build in systems to check important details. Sometimes the solution is to get someone else who likes details to do it. It is better to figure out how you can best manage your weaknesses than to avoid them. Then you can better focus on your strengths.

I know several entrepreneurs who immediately delegate the accounting to a bookkeeper because they said they were terrible at numbers and details. Over the years, and sometimes through a few failed businesses, they found it was better to have more concern, respect and knowledge for the numbers than they originally wanted. It was okay to delegate the accounting, but they also needed to know what was going on with the numbers on a regular basis. They understood that they could not be terrible at it if they wanted to succeed, nor could they entirely delegate it either. It was too much of a daily concern. They found they had to show some forethought and knowledge, or they could easily lose money without being aware of it. Plus, the accountant would yell at them for receipts, the government would question them, and audits would be forthcoming. If they wanted to avoid hassle, they had to get better at these things so that they could focus on their strengths, which were often at the other end of the spectrum, in people, ideas, and creativity. However, some of these successful people, after going through this process, found they were actually not bad with numbers and could see a whole new value to them. They found that cataloguing details and keeping up systems could save time in information retrieval. They found that details and numbers could be effective management and measurement tools, able to show when, where and how much they were succeeding. This didn't mean they came to love data entry, but they did better understand the thoughts behind knowledge management and retrieval, and the importance of it. They chose to let go of their mythologies of themselves, or change them to include a new skill. It may never be their strength, but it had become an asset.

I have seen others that lost tens of thousands of personal dollars to disorganization with a refusal to get in and learn something new, because of their mythologies of what they could and could not do. They usually created the mythology without ever having really tried to get better at the thing they chose to avoid. Again, people often change only when there is a crisis or when they need to, and some not even then, so strong is the desire to stick to a mythology. Some general mythology phrases people tell themselves and others that may hold them back are:

- "That's not for me"
- "I'm not a joiner"
- "I don't need to do that stuff"
- "I'll work it out by myself"
- "It will take too long to get that education"
- "It is too expensive"
- "I can't ask for money for that"
- "I am not a volunteer type"
- "I tried that once ten years ago and it didn't work"

□ "I'm too old, I can't change" (Scrooge actually says this before he is later convinced to change)

And there are so many more I hear people use everyday. My favorite ones on the list above are, "I'm not a joiner" and "It will take too long to get that education." Sometimes I interview people and find out what they are interested in but they say that they are not going to get the appropriate education or training to follow that interest because it will take two years, four years, or six years. I do understand that people have to make an opportunity-cost analysis -- that is, they have to decide if it is going to be worth the expense to put in that much time -- but often the most ironic and sad thing happens. That is, we hear that same person two, four or six years later in the same situation, making the same complaints about their life. It's easy to see that they could have had that degree or certificate by now and be starting their exciting new career, if they had stopped making an excuse about how long it was going to take.

The other one, "I am not a joiner" is also a very sad mythology. There are so many doors that are closed for the person with this attitude, when they could choose to open them but won't. One has to ask, what negative experience did they have in a group? Was it an early trauma? Were they forced to join something they hated?

Was the boy scouts or girl scouts too regimented for them? Are they resigned to introversion because it is comfortable? Do they just hate the hassles of working things out with others? In that case, they are denying themselves some basic life and leadership skills. We keep growing because others stimulate that growth. We have to respond to the people around us. When you cut yourself off from opportunities to work with others on a common interest, you cut yourself off from potential growth. Many stay stuck this way. Many stay in survival.

Exercise

What mythologies are you hanging on to, and repeating, that may affect your career, your relationships and your life? In the lists below choose as many items as you want in the relationship list and the career list, and write out your beliefs about each. Write down what you have heard yourself say or think in the past. There are blank spaces to add your own mythologies (the topics are not so important). Later, look through and analyze where this mythology may not be true. It may be what you choose to believe and if so, is it holding you back?

Relationship Mythology Topics	What's Your Mythology about…	Is it True? Is it holding you back?
True Love		
My First Love		
About My Last Relationship		
About My Current Relationship		
In order to be happy in a relationship I have to be…		
In order to be happy in a relationship they have to be…		
In order to be attracted to someone they have to…		
The most important thing in a relationship for me is…		
A Kiss		
Saying I love you		
A First date		
The Third date		
Sex		
Cuddling		

Career Mythology Topics	What's Your Mythology about….	Is it True? Is it holding you back?
Leadership		
Public Speaking		
Your ability to be hired		
If you are going to be fired it will be because…		
Detail-oriented		
Math, Accounting and numbers oriented		
Planning events		
Networking/Joining Groups		
Education/Training		
Computers/Tech		
Getting Your Hands Dirty		
Teamwork		
Dress and Grooming		
Travel		

For me, if I had done this exercise a number of years ago I would have put under the True Love Mythology: "True Love is a fairy tale." Now I believe the opposite. True love is a realistic goal that we should search for and strive for. Finding in yourself someone who is "true" and capable of both loving and of being loved is to find love that "cannot remove, nor be removed." Think of the "True" in True Love not only in the sense of being honest with yourself and others, but true in the same way a wheel runs true: stable, upright and spinning easily. These are characteristics to look for in yourself and in others. When it is True Love, it is stable love, it is honest love, and it is love that is easier. The point is, I certainly do believe in True Love now. I don't know what I thought it was before, which is the point. All I knew was that for me "True Love" was a roll-your-eyes kind of phrase. It was not something to believe in. It was a negative. When I let go of that mythology and the accompanying attitude, True Love was able to enter my life in many forms, from self-love, friends, creative expression, and a loving partner.

Occasionally, people discover that there are contradictions or conflicts in the mythologies they hold. Sometimes it is between career and relationship lists which keep them stuck in career vs. relationship. For example, when this exercise was done by a man I worked with he said that the most important aspect of relationship was "loyalty," yet under "last relationship" he said "too clingy." Under "travel for career" he said "I love to travel for work." It turns out that when he traveled for work, he was denying his last partner's desire to see more of him. Therefore, when he was in town, the love-starved partner was found to be "too clingy" by him. But he did admit that loyalty was important, since in a very early relationship infidelity of his partner had been a factor and he could not stomach that again. You can see that if he wants both loyalty and freedom, then he is in a contradiction with himself, and he is using work travel to keep distance in the relationship. Understanding this can underline the changes in mythologies need to take place so that there is no longer these conflicts.

Career *and* Relationships

The topics of career and relationship both deserve entire books on their own, and Lord knows there are many of them out there. Many of you may have valid reasons why you have not found the right career or the right person. You are doing many beneficial things and you continue to look; you have a great attitude and you just haven't found the career yet, or the person yet. All you need is that all-important persistence. In this chapter all I wanted to do was touch on a common phenomenon I have noticed that people set the two of the most important aspects of their lives, career and relationship so that they oppose one another, as in Career <u>vs</u>. Relationship. Though we have gone through only a handful of reasons why career and/or relationship may not be working out for a person, you should find that working on any of the areas this book mentions, such as self-esteem, will automatically positively affect your career and relationship. And the upcoming chapter on Focus and Persistence will give you the last key to thriving.

To recap this chapter:

- ☐ People have a strong tendency to link up with other people who are avoiding the other principal focus (career or relationship).
- ☐ You cannot grow or thrive if you do not look at what you are avoiding (either career of relationship, or both).
- ☐ People often want to be taken care of, or avoid being taken care of, and either extreme may interfere with the managing of their career or relationship, so that they cannot have both successfully.
- ☐ Accept the possibility that if you have had a career focus, then nurturing yourself to become a great, stable relationship person can give you the power to take greater risks in all aspects of your life, including your career.

☐ Accept the possibility that if you have had a relationship focus, then finding a vocation gives you more financial health and stability, and therefore more peace than you can find solely in a relationship. It will also make you more attractive to others.

☐ Getting through difficult times, builds a bond and greater trust with others. So don't give up on your relationships or your career because of the struggles alone; you may be on the verge of growing a little deeper or towards a good to great company, or a good to great relationship.

☐ Finding an ideal relationship or career isn't a question of simply finding the right person, company or field, it is a question of willingness to do something better than you ever have before.

☐ Some of the stories and truths you have been telling yourself are not truths, and neither are they lies. What they are is beliefs that you have chosen, which can hold you back. Be prepared to re-examine the popular mythologies which you have about yourself, your history and important aspects of life.

Chapter 9 - Focus and Persistence

Myths and Truths about Focus and Persistence

We've all heard them, the stories of people who knew what they want, often early in life, went after it and got it. These stories reinforce that we should know what we want, focus on it, and persist until we have it. Only then will the doors swing wide and welcome you to your personal Valhalla, the exclusive club of the successful, never to look back. In fact, some examples I've used in this book may seem just like such stories except there is a wrinkle that we get confused about. That wrinkle is that focus and persistence don't always go together at the same time. And that's reality. Let's take apart some of the myths and the truths of focus and persistence.

MYTH #1: You have to focus on just one thing in order to be successful

I am told that the most expensive coffee in the world is from coffee beans swallowed by wild civet cats in Malaysia. The cats then poop out the beans and they are brewed up to make a superior tasting cup of Java. This is called Kopi Luwak coffee and costs approximately $600 a pound.   Most of us - no matter how much we love our cup of Joe - are not going to be drinking Kopi Luwak. Likewise, every fresh-brewed myth has an appealing aroma, but sniff a little closer and there is often an undercurrent of the smell of fresh crap. The trouble with thinking that you have to focus on only one thing is that most people don't know what they want to do. They don't know what they should focus on. These are the people who identify that they are in Survival and are trying to struggle towards Thrival. Because they can't find or decide what they want, they describe themselves as stuck, and often tormented. They read books on focusing your goals, they get lots of advice from friends and partners, they sometimes do expensive tests, they may get coaching, and they may even narrow it down, but they never feel a certainty and they never shake that how-can-I-be-sure-feeling.

The truth is, that if you interview "successful" thriving people in your life; people who are happy, healthy and thriving, you will see that they did not necessarily start off focusing on one thing for their chosen occupation. Often they are just as surprised as anyone else at what became their occupation or passion in life. For every one person who knew what they wanted, focused on it and went after it, there are ten stories of people who kind of fell into what they do. They simply tried out many different things and "one thing led to another." The word "serendipity" was created just for this recurring phenomenon in our lives. My message is: don't fret if you don't know what you want to do. Don't feel you have to know before you try other things. Instead, figure out easy ways to "sample" things you think you may be interested in. Try things out, knowing you can give them up if they are not suiting you. By letting go of the myth of one thing to the exclusion of all others, you can embrace letting one thing lead to another. That is what sailors do. We don't all have the gas to power through. You are allowed to change your course, to see where the wind takes you and enjoy the journey.

Will you eventually settle on something if you let one thing lead to another? Perhaps. Or perhaps you will just have more than one kind of occupation in your life, and you can consider that lucky, too. As a human resources professional I have often seen the workaholic who cannot handle the idea of retiring, or refuses to retire even though they are using outdated work methods. They have never nurtured any interests or enjoyments outside their work. They have nothing that they can fall back on. Often, they have lost touch with their spouse. Sometimes they have no spouse or close companions outside of work. What does this mean? Too much of one thing, even if you enjoy it, can paint you into a corner later in life, or even before later life. Retirement, while it may be appropriate for an individual who is no longer thriving at their job anymore, can be a terrifying idea for them because they have psychologically set themselves up to do one thing. So, if you haven't found that one thing that you feel you can commit to, maybe you are luckier than you think. Instead of beating yourself up that you have missed the boat, perhaps you should enjoy the variety that you have chosen, or the potential to steer the boat in new directions.

MYTH #2 – The more things you do the more things you can do, and keeping this up is good

As I have said before all myths have a kernel of truth in them. This myth is sort of true and follows the same idea as that old expression, "if you want to get something done, ask a busy person to do it." Yes, the more things you do, the better you can get at multi-tasking. And the more hooks you keep in the water, the more you feel that you will get a nibble. However, this can lead to the opposite pitfall from focusing on only one thing. Instead, you may be trying to keep too many things going simultaneously. The question I would have you ask yourself is: Are these things all for you and what you care about, or are they mostly for others? Are you the busy person people ask to help them with their projects? The danger on the opposite side of focus is called spreading yourself too thin. It is dangerous, not only because you often end up not doing anything well, but also because you are doing things that contribute to others' goals instead of your own. This is not necessarily a bad thing, because it can help you discover your strengths and interests. But use that information for yourself, rather than getting stuck in a cycle of giving your time away. Consider a little reflection on the following things:

- Which things made you the most money?
- Which things did you give away?
- Which things did you enjoy doing?
- Which things could you never tire of doing?
- Which of the things you enjoy are in demand?
- What skills did you learn that you enjoy and that will transfer into something that is in demand?

Being an action-oriented person is great, but a little thought before and after action may make the rewards of your doer lifestyle much more fruitful and less exhausting.

MYTH #3 – Persistence and Focus go hand in glove for success

Again, all myths have truth to them. And all myths have a bit of cat poop. Persistence is a beautiful thing, and there's no denying that focus with persistence has allowed people to accomplish some pretty amazing things. But it is time to go back to Mr. Scrooge. No one can deny that Scrooge had focus and persistence. We also must now admit that focus and persistence kept him away from thriving until his miraculous night with the spirits. Sometimes it is better to stop persisting. Sometimes it is just wise to say "Que sera sera" and leave it up to a higher power, or to others. Sometimes tunnel vision accompanies so much focus and persistence. When that happens, it is wise to return to other joys, or at least take a break. This is known as figuring out what's truly important.

Persistence can be a wonderful thing as long as it doesn't take you too far away from what you intended. Buying our first property in Mexico, Jim, and I, ran into all kinds of unexpected snags. Pretty soon, we had been talked into side deals, schemes, and promises, all designed to get the house we wanted. And we were persistent.

Stupidly so. My exact words were "I am going to get that house come hell or high water." But all the wheeling and dealing got so far away from our original values of community and win-win that we needed to bring it back to a place of sanity and stop focusing solely on getting *that* house and *that* land in *that* area. As soon as we stopped ruthlessly persisting and focusing only on that one thing, a plethora of other possibilities entered our brains. Soon, we had not only a Plan A, but Plans B, C and D, all of which looked sensible and fitting. In the process we had learned a lot about buying real estate in other countries, even more than the people we thought of as experts. From this experience, Jim created a new career path helping other people buy real estate in Mexico (let one thing lead to another). Persistence is a beautiful thing but knowing when to walk away, even if you are taking some losses, is a beautiful thing too.

Not Just A Myth: Are You Suffering from FMS?

After examination of the two attributes of focus and persistence, it is hard to decide if you can always count on either attribute as being inherently honorable. However, focus lies very close to commitment, and without commitment you can fall victim to a vicious social disease call FMS: Fear of Missing Something. We all know numerous people who have this condition. In these days of rampant technology FMS has spread like a Trojan Horse computer virus. People may appear to have more choices, but in truth they allow themselves to *see* more choices. They want to see more choices in case – you guessed it – they might miss something. Ultimately, it is true they might miss something, but, we are always missing things, that is the nature of life. However, by not focusing on quality-of-now moments, what are FMS-conditioned people sacrificing?

FMS is inability to commit. I know people who cannot commit to a date or an invitation because they are afraid something better may come along. As a result they never get to know one individual, group, or organization in a deep way. Others cannot commit to putting their cell phones and blackberries aside long enough to have a focused conversation with others. What can this do to relationships? I will suggest that people quickly learn not to depend on an FMS person for important listening or anything important to them. They figure out that to the FMS individual they may be the flavor-of-the-moment and will be tossed aside when something or someone better comes along. Therefore, they return the favor by keeping them at the edge of their life. Deeper relationships never form. Managers intuitively may not rate an FMS as person as highly as others, because they see this person as someone who doesn't do each task thoroughly. They can be someone who tries to get a whole lot of everything done instead of prioritizing. People who suffer from extensive FMS may have crises late in life when they are figuring out they have been alienating people for years and the damage is not easily repaired.

It can affect one-on-one relationships but it can also affect relationships in a group. Every company, volunteer organization, classroom or club sees turnover. Sometimes turnover has a positive aspect of the process of getting the right people, but one sometimes wonders about those who are always drifting through and never staying for long. FMS can affect the depth of what you get out of being a member of any group. We have a motto in my Toastmasters Club: "You get out what you put in." People who opt out of committing for perhaps the wrong reasons (it wasn't exciting enough, easy enough, convenient enough, etc.) don't figure out how to meet challenges, cooperate, accomplish tasks or negotiate politics. These are things you learn when you work in groups. These are critical thrival skills. Thriving exists when a person embraces interdependence as well as independence. If we are too independent we can become an island, like Scrooge, but interdependence is finding community, and being a member of a community requires commitment, as the new Scrooge demonstrates.

If you have a bad case of FMS, you need not wonder why you feel like some days you are spinning your wheels in life. FMS will rob you of focus, commitment, persistence and connection with others, which are all ingredients you need in the right balance in order to thrive. You may feel edgy and less satisfied, always hoping for something better rather than fully being in the moment.

To recap this chapter:

- ☐ You don't have to find just one thing to be successful – experiment and let one thing lead to another.
- ☐ Spreading yourself too thin means you need to ask yourself some Why questions.
- ☐ Try to do more of the things that gain you one, or all, of the following things: 1) develop in-demand or practical skills, 2) give you enjoyment or fulfillment, 3) help accomplish your goals.
- ☐ Sometimes you have to let go of things and not resist tunnel vision persistence – remind yourself what really matters.
- ☐ If you have FMS (Fear of Missing Something) you may want to consider how you are being perceived in a negative non-committal light and how it affects your relationships.
- ☐ If you have FMS you may want to consider what your lack of commitment prevents you from developing.

Chapter 10 – Forward to Thrival

Firing on All Cylinders: Asking For and Getting Help

My partner, Jim, likes to say, "When are we going to start firing on all cylinders?" Which means, when are we going to reach our full potential and use all of our resources to the max? Most people never do. Most people use less than one tenth of their resources, internal and external. They don't recognize them, or if they do, they have many excuses why they are not using them. Because it does take effort, it is often easier to blame someone, make excuses to stay in victim mentality and not thrive. However, many important breakthroughs are attained by using persistence in looking for help.

In this section are lists of internal resources and external resources. Internal resources are your own abilities or potential, should you choose to use them. External resources are all the people and organizations out there that are willing to help you. You may want to scan ahead to get a sense of what these resources are.

Sometimes people see external resources as taking too long, jumping through too many hoops, coming with strings attached, or without immediate pay-offs. They are right. There are no guarantees that everything you put effort into will pay off soon or in the way you wanted. Ask any salesman. Getting assistance for yourself can be, and should be, a successive process. However, if you are persistent, you will usually succeed and it may be much easier than you thought. Also, many happy serendipitous occurrences happen en route when people show persistence in trying to get some help. Other resources, opportunities and solutions often seem to magically appear just because you have made a commitment to moving forward and reaching out.

If you are aware of resources that may help you, but are not trying them, ask yourself if your reasons for not going forward are valid, or are they excuses? Do you have fears? What are they? If you think they are valid reasons, can you find another resource instead? There are many resources out there. Is the root of the problem that you do not like asking for help, or accepting help? Do you have a belief that taking assistance of any kind shows weakness or dependence? As stated before, men have a tendency to go into counseling - ask for help - only when they are in a crisis or have already lost something. Women, on the other hand, tend to go into counseling because they want to improve their lives or they want to get something. However, either gender can shy away from getting help when they could use it to move them forward. Many still feel like we should be able to figure it all out by ourselves. It is important to break away from these blocks, if we are to start firing on all cylinders.

Many people find they like to have a coach, to help them focus and keep them on track, strengthen their habits, and help them get over their fears. We would not expect Olympic athletes to go into competition without coaches. Why short change yourself from a high performance thriving life? My first coach was one of the most exclusive and expensive coaches in the city, yet I didn't pay a cent. By chance we met at a networking event and struck up a conversation and realized that we could work out a barter deal, where I gave her some coaching on writing and she gave me life skills coaching. You may work with a coach who is just starting out, or does a sliding scale in order to fit it in your budget. Most reputable coaches do a first session free and charge only if there seems to be a good fit, and a mutual agreement to go forward. If it seems like a great expense when you find out the minimum charge is $90 an hour in many cases (and that may be just for phone) consider that you can get way more bang for your buck if you focus the sessions on one aspect of your life you want to improve first. Good coaches always give homework and usually do some sort of assessment of you in some way, be it a questionnaire, in depth interview or even a test. This way if you don't have a focus they will likely work with you in an impartial way to find that focus. Remember, if you want to go to the Olympics it would be unthinkable not to have a coach.

That was my pitch for coaching, but what if a coach is not for you? You could start your own Thrival Group to move you towards successive progress (find out how at www.survivaltothrival.com). Work together on the exercises in this book. Start with small things and use each other as a positive buddy system. Your significant relationships are important in the process of thriving. Putting yourself in positive environments with positive people at work, home or play, is crucial to your success. Surrounding yourself with positive people and remaining supportive and positive yourself will move you towards success, however you have come to define it.

Exercise

Become aware of your internal and external resources and start to incorporate more of them in your life. By doing this, you will soon be firing on all cylinders and make the rest of us look like we are standing still. Use these lists below to understand how much you have going for you.

Internal Resources

You are going to want to remind yourself of these and nurture and develop them always. Check which ones you want to strengthen, and circle the ones you know are your strong suits that you can build from:

- ☐ Ability not to be a victim or think like one
- ☐ Ability to leave the past behind
- ☐ Many talents you personally have – list them!
- ☐ Some kind of willpower or discipline you showed (what was it?)
- ☐ Ability to stick with something until you've accomplished it (what did you stick with?)
- ☐ Ability to take care of yourself (how do you do this?)
- ☐ Things in your life that make you happy now (what are they?)

- ☐ Ability to love yourself
- ☐ Ability to ask for help or know when you can use help
- ☐ Choices – you always have the ability to make a choice in everything
- ☐ You want things to be better
- ☐ Your intuition
- ☐ Your experience and wisdom
- ☐ Ability to let go of things or let things go
- ☐ Ability to nurture and maintain friendships
- ☐ Ability to have intimate conversations
- ☐ Ability to trust
- ☐ Ability to teach
- ☐ Ability to learn
- ☐ Ability to nurture others
- ☐ Ability to lead
- ☐ Ability to follow good leaders
- ☐ Ability to receive compliments (just say thank you)
- ☐ Your values
- ☐ Ability to meditate
- ☐ Ability to keep a journal
- ☐ Your honesty
- ☐ Your willingness
- ☐ Ability to find purpose and meaning in your life
- ☐ Ability to form your own support groups

- ☐ Ability to make new friends
- ☐ Your creative imagination
- ☐ Your smile
- ☐ Ability to make lists
- ☐ Your good health
- ☐ Ability to network and join groups.

Perhaps there are some internal resources you need to nurture. Find out how best to do that and who can help you. Some of the "who" may be listed in your external resources listed below.

External resources

Resources you should take advantage of:

- ☐ Supportive & wise friends, family and buddies – list them!
- ☐ Pets to love when humans are difficult
- ☐ Books & literacy – you can read!
- ☐ Audio Books & Videos
- ☐ Libraries – free knowledge, books, lectures, resources, events, opportunities!
- ☐ Courses: schools, colleges, universities, technical institutes, night schools, etc.

- ☐ Recreation centers -- cheap education and fitness resources that can be top quality
- ☐ Non-profit associations
- ☐ 12-Step Groups -- in addition to AA, there are now 12-step peer groups on nearly every kind of addiction
- ☐ Professional addiction recovery organizations
- ☐ Professional associations
- ☐ Clubs --Toastmasters or other specialty clubs that do not cost a lot to join
- ☐ Coaches
- ☐ Counselors
- ☐ Grief counselors
- ☐ Health professionals
- ☐ Communities (of all kinds)
- ☐ Artist's groups – join or form your own -- start that garage band!
- ☐ Churches
- ☐ Choirs
- ☐ 1-800 help-lines
- ☐ Tax breaks -- know them and take advantage
- ☐ Workplace benefits plans
- ☐ EAP – Employee Assistance Programs – (most work places that have health benefits now have EAPs – ask!) they provide counseling and other resources for you and your family on

many personal subjects from buying a house to finding daycare
to relationship counseling

☐ Acquaintances

☐ Kind strangers

☐ Neighbors

☐ Parenting groups and resources

☐ Camps for kids, teens and adults

☐ Charities

☐ Mentors

☐ Good bosses

☐ Networking groups

☐ Social groups

☐ Teachers

☐ The Internet for finding all these resources and researching
areas of interest or concern, or using internet chat groups -
Go to www.survivaltothrival.com!

☐ Stories you hear that help you, or stories you repeat that
help you

☐ Positive media stories and helpful information you get via
TV, newspapers or magazines

☐ Employment insurance (unemployment insurance)

☐ Government agencies/departments and programs

☐ Social assistance (Welfare) and associated programs – no
shame no blame

☐ Back-to-work programs

☐ Self-employment or entrepreneurship programs

☐ Insurance

☐ Scholarships

☐ Student loans

☐ Grants

☐ Personal assets (money or things that translate into cash)

☐ Possessions

☐ Bartering groups

☐ Nature

☐ Parks

☐ Cheap transportation options

☐ Free give-aways, consignment stores, craigslist, etc.

☐ Activism and political groups

☐ Software programs or downloadable programs from the internet: shareware and freeware!

☐ Fitness groups

☐ Sports of all kinds

☐ Sports groups, leagues and associations

☐ Personal trainers

☐ Housing organizations

☐ Co-operatives of all kinds

There are, of course, many more. If you are truly someone who can fire on all cylinders you should be able to say you have used almost every one of the resources on the above list at one time or another. You should also be able to say you are continuing to use some resources all of the time. If you haven't used a large number of them, start. *Check off* the ones you haven't yet tried. *Star* the ones you think you should try and that are appropriate for where you are right now in your life. And, go back to resources you've forgotten about and think you could benefit from again. Use your judgment. You may choose resources that require greater commitment and focus, knowing that they are the ones that will benefit you most in the long run. Some will be short-term, but have lasting effects. If you can't find the right help, keep looking. Use that persistence. Once you have found some good resources, choose ones that bring you benefits right now, ones that help towards a future goal, and ones that will provide on-going learning and development.

History repeatedly demonstrates that the people who learn how to use the resources around them most effectively move from survival to thrival. Often this meant natural resources, but as humans have grown more sophisticated, different kinds of resources from knowledge to personal growth. I know that human beings who focus on getting the best kind of resources, and persist in developing themselves, usually achieve the success they are looking for.

Stay in Your Comfort Zone: Finding Community

Have you ever read a self-help book where the author says: "stay in your comfort zone?" It is practically a cliché to tell you to "step outside your comfort zone". Even I have asked you to challenge your comfort zone. But I am going to reverse that. This may be a first, but it is true that it is okay to stay with things that are within comfortable reach. Sometimes it is best to start with, or even stay with, the low hanging fruit. Just as would-be writers are advised to "write what you know," and just as Warren Buffet says he "won't invest in anything he doesn't understand," staying with the things you know is one of the many paths a person can take to thrival - Did I mention there is more than one path?

There is no one single path to thrival, and yours may be either comfortable or challenging, but I don't know anyone who thrives without being surrounded by what can be described as community. In this contemporary world of over-population, late-capitalism, secularism, the automobile and the jet plane, we don't have communities in the same way we once did. People have to seek community if they want to gain the comfort and benefits of belonging. Communities should be the ultimate areas of comfort. Many of us belong to several communities. You may seek out an existing community or you may want to initiate your own. Where you find these communities is unimportant as long as they have the qualities of a healthy community.

A Healthy Community:
- ☐ Has a place or places that members habitually return to (a physical or virtual location or locations)
- ☐ Has a location that is cared for and respected but is rarely the focus of the community
- ☐ Has a focus or focuses that bring them together on a regular basis
- ☐ Has a focus that can be described as healthy and helpful
- ☐ Has a written or unwritten agenda to look out for their members' well-being (support them)
- ☐ Has roles that each member takes and may fulfill either in the location or away from it
- ☐ Has expectations of its members, beyond just showing up
- ☐ Has formal or informal leaders
- ☐ Has values and guidelines that vary in complexity from common courtesy to complex rules, procedures and regulations

☐ Has power to displace members who are seen to threaten the purpose of the community, or threaten the well-being of other members

☐ May be open to all or has attainable guidelines for entrance

☐ Regularly welcomes new members, without prejudice

☐ Keeps connections with the outside world and does not try to control its members outside relationships, activities or lives (is not cult-like)

What you gain from being a community member is:

☐ A sense of purpose

☐ Regular connections to others: relationships

☐ Strength in numbers and organized mobility (many hands make light work)

☐ Social life, friends and fun (whether it is intended or not)

☐ Sense of propriety

☐ Healthy structure and routine

☐ People you are accountable to

☐ A place where you are accepted, valued and supported

☐ A place where opportunities may be open to you

☐ A place where knowledge and ideas are disseminated

☐ A place where you can share with others: skills, knowledge, aid, participation, growth, etc.

☐ A sense of safety, comfort and belonging

Make a list of all the communities you belong to and what you gain from them. Like a popular ad on the television says, "you may be richer than you think." But if you don't think you are getting what you need from the communities you already have, you may want to seek other communities (see external resources list), or create a community. If seeking other communities or creating one moves you out of your comfort zone, don't fret, if you find the right community and stay in it, you will find that it will become your ultimate comfort zone. And that is a good thing.

The Gratitude Cycle

Do you remember back in Chapter Three when I talked about attitudes and entitlement? I want to revisit those ideas to get to another important concept: The Gratitude Cycle.

Attitudes that keep people from thriving are:

- ☐ I don't deserve it
- ☐ I am entitled to it (I not only deserve it, but I shouldn't have to do anything more to get it, it should come easily)

All of us spring back and forth between these attitudes without really noticing, and we do it all the time. Daily and even moment by moment we can feel underlying feelings of both unworthiness and entitlement. What we could be aiming towards, that may make this ping-ponging of opposing feelings unnecessary, is understanding what I call The Gratitude Cycle. The Gratitude Cycle reinforces the feeling you do deserve things you have worked towards or wished for, but it also includes being grateful for whatever comes to you, even if it is not at all what you wanted.

Being grateful is a way to thwart bitterness and suffering and to actually help bring good things to you. How this works is one of the great mysteries of life. Acceptance of defeating, disappointing or even horrible facts is one of the most difficult challenges of all. Some say there are things that happen which have no silver linings. But I would say even the most difficult of challenges, even the most horrible of events, comes with lessons to be learned and possibilities for greater compassion. Some men like Bettelheim and Frankl, who survived to write about the concentration camps of Nazi Germany, gained valuable understanding of human nature that they were able to share and use in compassionate practices, philosophies and teachings. Although the hands we are dealt may be less extreme than being interned in barbaric prisons, all our challenges contain lessons and growth.

But if The Gratitude Cycle only counted on you finding silver linings and being grateful it would not be as powerful as it is. The Gratitude Cycle counts on you making an effort.

The Gratitude Cycle isn't linear. It is better described as a wheel. But for the purposes of explanation, I've listed seven steps.

1. You want or need something.
2. You spend time telling people what you want and accept help that is offered.
3. You put effort towards getting what you want, or searching for what you want, and this effort must connect in some way to the outside world (although visualizing is very powerful, wishing is not enough).
4. You stop your efforts when you run out of steam or have exhausted all possibilities, and simply wait for something to come back to you. Move on to something else.
5. When it does come back, you are grateful even when it's not what you expected. If it seems like bad news, learn from it and reevaluate what you want. Decide if a change of course is required or greater persistence. If it is something good, understand that you are deserving of it, but also grateful.
6. Be grateful for people and things you already have.
7. Help others get what they need or want.

As you can see the wheel is just as easily and logically started from #6. Be grateful for people and things you already have, or #7. Help others get what they want or need. Some of us may be overly comfortable helping others; others may have trouble with satisfying others before ourselves. It doesn't matter where you start as long as you move through all the stages at some point. This cycle is also somewhat like "what goes around, comes around" but with a little more clarity and understanding.

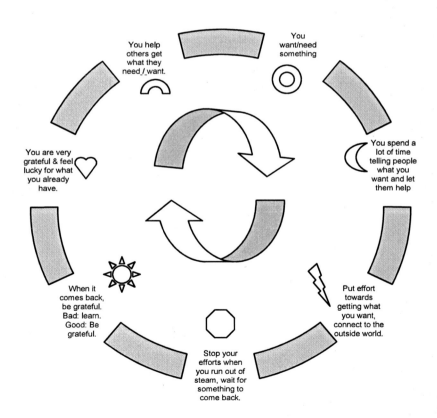

Why is it important to incorporate The Gratitude Cycle if you truly want to thrive? Because we don't have time to waste on bitterness and unhappiness. By being grateful for what happens, no matter what happens, you will help good things to happen, or as the late great Mae West used to say, "Don't spend too much time crying over a man [or woman], the next one may fall for your smile." Be grateful to the universe and it tends to smile on you.

The Final Word

This book has given you an abundance of ideas and techniques to start you on your own path to thrival. Please do not freeze up at the idea that there is so much to "work on." Don't feel you have to do it all or even part of it. Leave the exercises undone. There is only one important thing I want you to take away from this book and that is the message in Chapter Four.

Self-esteem is not something that you acquire once and it stays forever. It is an on-going process of reminding yourself that you are worthy of love and respect and that you can give it to yourself. It is a constant process of forgiving your mistakes, transforming your negative words and thoughts about yourself to positive ones, telling yourself you love yourself, and truly accepting yourself for the wonderful you that you are. Remember that it is worth making that kind of effort towards greater self-esteem. When you consciously raise your own level of self-esteem, you will find that all else, whatever you are seeking, will often fall in place effortlessly.

To go back to Scrooge one last time, if Dickens created a character who discovered that kindness to others was more important than money, he also created a character who returned to his community, and not only began loving others again but -- as old as he was -- also began truly loving himself and the gift of life itself for perhaps the first time in his life.

To recap this chapter:
- □ Firing on All Cylinders means developing your ability to find resources externally and internally and to get help.
- □ Getting out of your comfort zone does not have to be uncomfortable if you find a supportive community.
- □ In the Gratitude Cycle it is important that you discuss with others things you want and then take concrete actions towards attaining goals (not just thinking, wishing or "manifesting").

- ☐ In the Gratitude Cycle it is important that you are grateful for whatever comes back to you and the lessons you can take from it.

- ☐ In the Gratitude Cycle it is important that you offer to give to others without wanting anything in return.

- ☐ The most important Thrival skill is to build and maintain your self-esteem. It is an on-going Thrival practice that will take constant reinforcement.

To access *Survival to Thrival* assessments, books, blogs, events, coaching, training, support groups, workshops…

go to:

survivaltothrival.com

The Tenets to Thriving

- ☐ Always expect things to change whether you want them to or not.
- ☐ Take an attitude of full accountability, without blaming either yourself or others.
- ☐ Don't ignore the Elephant in the Livingroom.
- ☐ Love yourself always.
- ☐ Support and encourage others, and keep supportive people around you.
- ☐ Question people, but don't try to change them.
- ☐ Health and happiness for mind, body, pocketbook and soul can be attended to simultaneously.
- ☐ Speak with a power of choice and not limitation or despair.
- ☐ Get rid of old mythologies that no longer serve you.
- ☐ Create new positive habits as the antidote to fear.
- ☐ Take and seek help: Fire On All Cylinders.
- ☐ Be grateful and appreciative.

To access *Survival to Thrival* assessments, books, blogs, events, coaching, training, support groups, workshops… go to:

survivaltothrival.com

END NOTES

[i] *Prescriptions for Happiness?* by <u>Seymour Fisher</u>, <u>Roger P. Greenberg</u>, Publication: Psychology Today
Publication Date: Sep/Oct 95, (Document ID: 1266)
Summary: Are antidepressants helping, or is it the power of positive thinking?

[ii] University of Toronto news release, 2008, *Postnatal Depression Prevented without Drugs*, study of 701 high-risk mothers.

[iii] *Depression is a Choice: Winning the Battle without Drugs*, A.B. Curtiss, Hyperion, New York, 2001

[iv] *Procrastination and Task Avoidance: theory, research and treatment* by Joseph Ferrari, Judith Johnson, Willian McCowan, Plenium Press, Springer, New York, 1995
[v] *The Dark Side of Sleeping Pills*, Dr. Daniel F. Kripke, paper published at the University of California, 2002

[vi] 'Maggie's Law: National Drowsy Driving Act of 2003', February 27, 2003 A bill to amend title 23, United States Code, to provide incentives to States for the development of traffic safety programs to reduce crashes related to driver fatigue and sleep deprivation.